NATURAL MONUMENTS OF

AMERICA

Donald Young

PORTLAND HOUSE

New York

This 1990 edition published by Portland House,
a division of dilithium Press, Ltd.,
distributed by Crown Publishers, Inc.,
225 Park Avenue South, New York, New York 10003.

Printed and Bound in Singapore

Library of Congress Catalog Card Number: 90-60562

ISBN 0-517-01503-X
hgfedcba

Author: Donald Young
Producer: Robert M. Tod
Designer and Art Director: Mark Weinberg
Editor: Michael Vickerman
Picture Research: Ede Rothaus and Grace How
Associate Art Director: Louise Sullivan

TABLE OF CONTENTS

A mother bear begs for food in Yellowstone in 1937. The Park Service now strongly discourages feeding of wildlife and other attempts to make contact with wild animals.

Introduction

February. The snow is deep and the air bitterly cold. It numbs your fingertips and crinkles the hairs in your nostrils. In front of you, steam and hot bubbly water rise from the ground. You are close enough to feel the warmth but far enough away to avoid being scalded.

The steam forms a white curtain before your eyes, but you soon realize that you are not alone. Deeper sounds, snorts and grunts, intrude on the hissing and cheerful whistling of the small geyser. Dark forms move beyond the curtain. Large black hairy beasts, their visible breath mingling with the steam, struggle through the snow. They have come to this spot to seek relief from the cold and to nibble on plants nourished by the heat of the geyser.

These are American bison, also called buffalo, and this is Yellowstone National Park in winter.

A store that sold camping equipment once had as its slogan, "Before you go, you dream." Next to the slogan was a drawing of a hiker wearing a pack and looking off into the distance. Dreams of wilderness adventure can still come true in the United States, and in fact those dreams had their beginning at Yellowstone, the first national park in the United States—and in the world as well.

Until the 17th century the future United States was, of course, one vast park. By then, Europe had been settled and the populations of Asia were filling up that continent. But the Western Hemisphere, though "discovered" by Columbus in 1492, remained largely unmarked by its relatively small number of Native inhabitants.

From the time Europeans began settling the East Coast in the early 1600s, the transformation of their adopted country occurred quickly. Whether fleeing political or religious persecution, or else lured by the prospect of better economic opportunities across the sea, they had chosen to make their home in the New World. And, as Professor Roderick Nash has written, "Wilderness, after all, was what had made the New World new."

But if wilderness offered the untrammeled freedom pioneers had never known in Europe, it also presented many dangers, including hostile Indians and wild animals. The wilds were also perceived as a barrier to "progress," by which was usually meant the opportunity to earn a living.

Hence, across the land, from the forests of New England, to the mountains and valleys of Appalachia, to the Midwest and to the edges of the Great Plains, the snap of an axe striking wood, followed by the splintering crash of a tree, carried from ridge to valley and signaled the arrival of civilization to once-virgin country. In the two-and-a-half centuries prior to 1872, when the first national park was proclaimed, most of the original American "park" had been chopped down and plowed over, and consequently, the creation of official parks were belated and imperfect attempts to preserve representative remnants of what had been pristine wilderness.

Settlers suffered no sense of loss in the toppling of trees. After all, there was always more untouched timber beyond the next river, wasn't there? Besides, it was written in the Bible that mankind should increase in numbers, conquer the earth, and have dominion over other creatures. God was clearly on the side of Paul Bunyan and the plowman. Alexis de Tocqueville, during a visit to frontier Michigan in 1831, found Americans on "the march across these wilds, draining swamps, turning the course of rivers, peopling solitudes, and subduing nature." The 1890 Federal census confirmed that the frontier had disappeared, that the United States had been occupied from coast to coast, albeit thinly in many areas. But attitudes had already begun to change. In dirty, crowded, rapidly growing cities, more citizens yearned to see something of what was left of the natural world, and actually wanted to experience the rugged outdoor life that their pioneer kinsmen had known. Many urban Americans had grown prosperous and had more free time than their country cousins. The concept of "vacation" had penetrated the American consciousness. From this class, the yuppies of their day, sprang the impetus for the creation of national parks.

Even before the 1890 census officially closed an era in American history, the preservation of parklands for posterity was well underway. Public gardens and city parks were an Old World feature adopted in the New. Then, in 1832, the artist George Catlin carried the concept of common ground a great step forward. Catlin, a serious student of American Indian life, contributed greatly to our appreciation of the first Americans through his writing, paintings, and engravings. In the spring of 1832 he had traveled to present-day South Dakota to paint scenes of the Sioux nation. But he was dismayed by what he saw. The Sioux had proved unable to cope with the arrival of white men. Many of them drank heavily, and killed buffalo in order to trade the hides for whiskey.

Catlin was convinced that something had to be done, quickly. After he spent some time looking out over the prairie, he wrote that much of the West was "worthy of our preservation and protection." He called for the creation of "a *magnificent park…a Nation's Park*, containing man and beast, in all the wild[ness] and freshness of their nature's beauty!"

In that same year, 1832, Congress approved the creation of the Hot Springs Reservation in Arkansas. At that site 47 hot springs spilled forth water from deep underground. People with various ailments were coming from long distances to bathe in the hot water in the hope that the experience might improve their health. In creating the reservation, the United States also established the principle that a natural feature was worth protecting. (Almost a century later, Hot Springs was redesignated as a national park.)

The occasional visionary such as Catlin was gradually joined by other Americans who questioned the unthinking despoliation of so much of the land. For one thing, some religious leaders had second thoughts about the Biblical sanction for taming the wild. They questioned whether God, the Creator of the universe and of all the plants and animals, wanted humans to overrun nature and bend it to their own convenience. They also argued that God showed His love for us through creation of the natural world.

The writer Henry David Thoreau thought we were losing something very important to us as we continued to chop down the forests. In 1851 he put it in eight beautiful words: "In wildness is the preservation of the world." He was convinced that opportunities to enjoy the ruggedness of nature would make all of us more alive, stronger in body and spirit.

Scientists spoke up, too. With the passing years, more young people were being trained as biologists and, botanists, and they urged that nature be preserved for scientific study. They realized that many species of plants and animals were becoming rare or even disappearing altogether.

And some thoughtful Americans began to ask themselves, What makes us different, special? The U.S. tradition of political and religious freedom was the most obvious answer. But Americans were also a little defensive. Europe's many cathedrals, museums and classical antiquities embodied a centuries-long cultural heritage. In contrast, America's cultural development was still in its infancy.

However, Americans had something Europeans did not have: a vast, sparsely populated country, with jagged mountain peaks, tumbling rivers, seemingly bottomless canyon gorges, and bountiful wildlife. Europe was fully populated, with only a few areas remaining in their natural state. And so, America's natural wonders could become its cathedrals, its monuments. In a land where no man can become king, the great western parks would some day commonly be called the crown jewels of the

United States.

In 1864 Congress gave Yosemite Valley to California and instructed the state to create a *state* park. In this way, formal protection was first given to the enchanting corridor through the High Sierras 150 miles east of San Francisco. Just a few years later, the world's first *national* park became a reality.

For decades grizzled prospectors and "mountain men" had explored the land near the headwaters of the Yellowstone River. When they went back East and told of seeing smoking fumaroles, geysers spewing hot water hundreds of feet in the air, and swirling pools of minerals in a rainbow of colors, people said they were delirious. But these and many other "rumors" from the West proved to be true.

The Federal government sent an expedition into the region in 1870, with civilians being escorted by the U.S. Cavalry. They gazed upon Yellowstone Falls, Yellowstone Lake, and the geyser basins. As the men on horseback emerged from a dense lodgepole pine forest and entered an open valley, a geyser "performed" for them as they approached it. They named it "Old Faithful." Today, this geyser remains the symbol of the park.

On the historic night of September 19, 1870, near the confluence of the Gibbon and Firehole rivers, the men sat around a campfire, discussing what they had seen. Several said that they intended to stake claims around the geysers so they could charge tourists who would pay to see them. But another man, Cornelius Hedges, later a judge in the Montana Territory, objected, arguing that Yellowstone "ought to be set apart as a great National Park." One of his companions at the campfire, Nathaniel P. Langford, lay awake that night thinking over the idea. Embracing the cause, he spent the next few months publicizing Yellowstone and urging Congress to approve a park. In doing so, he challenged the nearly universal assumption of the time that all of the public domain should be sold or given away.

Ferdinand Hayden, director of the Geological and Geographical Survey of the Territories, led a second expedition into the area in 1871. The painter Thomas Moran and the photographer William Henry Jackson went with him. Perhaps more than anything else, Jackson's photographs convinced Congress and the public that a park must be established. In 1872 Congress passed and President Ulysses S. Grant signed into law a bill that created Yellowstone National Park. The law described Yellowstone as "a public park or pleasuring ground for the benefit and enjoyment of the people."

Many Congressmen and newspaper writers had little understanding of the geological features that were being protected. They were often referred to as "curiosities," "decorations," and "freaks."

The automobile had not yet been invented, but the Northern Pacific Railroad had big plans for transporting tourists to the park, and it therefore became an enthusiastic supporter of Yellowstone. The Northern Pacific and other railroads sometimes pressed for commercial development inside the parks that was not always suitable for them. But the railroads deserve much of the credit for introducing the early parks to the American people.

In Yellowstone's early years, visitors had true wilderness experiences. In 1877 the Seventh Cavalry pursued the great leader Chief Joseph and his band of Nez Perce through the park. The Indians grabbed two groups of campers, including a number of women, and took them along. The Nez Perce later allowed their white captives to escape through a landscape of spouting geysers and bubbling mudpots.

Despite having been "protected," Yellowstone at first was anybody's park. Sportsmen shot bison and ranchers let their cattle graze within the park boundaries. Visitors teased the geysers, some even shaking soap flakes into the vents in hopes of provoking an eruption. In 1886 the Army was formally assigned responsibility for the park, and the soldiers chased out the poachers and squatters. Unfortunately, the military, which was also put in charge of other early parks, demonstrated little understanding of the forces of nature. Believing that tourists wanted to see the large herbivores such as elk and deer, the soldiers killed the wolves, coyotes, and mountain lions that preyed on them. In turn, the browsing and grazing animals, no longer menaced by predators, multiplied in number. They outgrew their food supply and perished in mass starvations. This tragic outcome was one of many painful lessons taught to humans who sought to "manage" nature.

The example of Yellowstone inspired railroads and other commercial interests banking on a profitable tourist trade to call for more parks. Such pressure, coupled with a growing public appetite for preserving the country's natural splendor, created a favorable climate in Congress for national park proposals. Today, 50 lovely remnants of the original America have been officially designated as national parks, but the efforts to establish them almost always met resistance.

In fact, a common pattern emerged, one in which a lone individual typically devoted years to promoting a particular landscape with which he had fallen in love. Getting approval of a park was almost always a struggle, and the conflicts featured a cast of characters that seldom varied except in name—articulate naturalists asserting that the nation would shame itself if it failed to create a park, corporations fulminating against "locking up" resource-rich land, lumbermen and miners lamenting the possible loss of jobs, logrolling Congressmen agreeing to support another's park bill in return for some other favor, and an occasional generous millionaire buying up acreage and presenting it to the government for a park. Sometimes schoolchildren contributing nickels and dimes played a supporting role.

Yellowstone is in the Rocky Mountains, principally in Wyoming. The next chapters of the national parks story would be written in California. John Muir, the prototypical lone crusader, a man willing, even eager, to devote his life to a single cause, would be the hero of those chapters.

Muir was born in Scotland, but his family emigrated to the United States, and he spent the rest of his boyhood in Wisconsin. He was a Christian—a Calvinist—and his religious training had nothing to say about protecting nature. But Muir studied geology and botany at the University of Wisconsin, and he found order and harmony in the natural world. In the wilderness, unimproved by "civilization," everything had a purpose. Where less perceptive people could see only chaos and confusion, Muir saw a grand design created by God. In Muir's words, every species is "hitched to everything else in the universe."

In 1867, at age 29, while working in a factory in Indianapolis, Muir nearly lost his sight in an accident. Believing that God was telling him that it was time for him to enter the wilderness, Muir struck out on his own, hiking a thousand miles to the Gulf of Mexico. Then he headed west, to San Francisco. Telling a passerby that his next destination was "any place that is wild," Muir entered the wilderness of the Sierra Nevada. *Sierra* is a Spanish word describing a mountain range that has jagged peaks. The range that runs through eastern California certainly fits that description.

When Muir first saw Yosemite Valley, it had already been made a state park. He immediately fell in love with the valley, and he would later write of "holy Yosemite." Millions of people now share Muir's belief that Yosemite Valley's seven miles offer the most lovely vista in the United States. During the Ice Age, thousands of years ago, mighty glaciers pushed through it and gouged out the broad U-shape. The high, hard, light gray granite walls of the valley convey a feeling of power and strength. Yet when you look at them, you do not feel overwhelmed, or menaced. They are perfectly designed, the magnum opus of a great sculptor.

In the spring, as the snow melts in the high country, misty waterfalls spill icy water hundreds of feet onto the valley floor. Deer and other animals feed in the grassy valley and drink from the Merced River, whose current runs swiftly from the mountains. At the upper end of the valley, Mirror Lake is so smooth that it contains a perfect mirror image of the mountains rising above it.

Muir explored the vast rugged mountain country above the valley. He was dismayed by the mess humans were making of the region. In the valley, inside the state park, hotels and other places of business had been built. Sheep—which he called "hoofed locusts"—and cattle ranged widely over the mountains, destroying and consuming wildflowers and other plants.

Muir, a skillful writer and promoter, resolved that the park at Yosemite must be expanded. Influential magazines published his articles. "Climb the mountains and get their good tidings," was his classic advice. "Nature's peace will flow into you as the sunshine into the trees. The winds will blow their freshness into you, and the storms their energy, while cares drop off like autumn leaves."

Muir's efforts, supported by others, finally paid off in 1890 when Congress approved a Yosemite National Park. The valley itself remained a state park until 1906, when the state returned it to Federal control for inclusion in the national park.

To Muir's delight, Congress established two more national parks in the Sierra Nevada in 1890. Sequoia and General Grant parks protected stands of the giant sequoia trees. Lumber companies had their eyes on the trees, the world's heaviest living things. Both parks were later expanded to protect more of the trees and the rugged mountain country of the Sierra Nevada. The Grant park later became part of Kings Canyon National Park.

Owners of sheep and cattle were outraged when their animals were banished from Yosemite National Park. They sought to abolish it, or at least to reduce its boundaries. Robert Underwood Johnson, an editor of *Century Magazine* who had published Muir's articles, feared that the California parks might be in danger. He suggested to Muir that an organization of private citizens be formed to help defend them. Muir welcomed the idea of a club that could "do something for wildness and make the mountains glad." Some California university professors also wanted to form a club.

This new organization, the Sierra Club, was founded in 1892. The club's 182 charter members elected Muir president, a position he held for 22 years until his death. In the early years, most Sierrans lived in California, and they focused primarily on exploring and protecting the Sierra Nevada range. Nowadays, with more than 500,000 members nationwide, the organization seeks to make the American people aware of many different threats to the environment, such as acid rain and toxic wastes.

The Sierra Club has won many victories over the years, but its first was one of its most important. It helped defeat an attempt by stockmen to reduce the size of Yosemite by one-half.

Two mountains created by volcanic eruptions became national parks at the turn of the century. The first, Mount Rainier, an ice-covered peak that soars above dense forests and flowered subalpine meadows southeast of Seattle, joined the list in 1899.

Crater Lake came next, and its eventual elevation to national park status provides a case study illustrating how one person can make a difference. One day in 1870, as a Kansas schoolboy eating his lunch at school, William Gladstone Steel glanced at the newspaper in which his mother had wrapped the food. It contained an article that told an incredible story. About seven thousand years ago in far-off Oregon, near the Pacific Ocean, a massive volcanic explosion had collapsed the mountaintop and sent ash spewing some 700 miles to the east. The sky must have been black for days. The explosion had left a crater inside the mountain, and inside the crater a beautiful deep blue lake had formed.

Steel decided he had to see that lake. Many years later, as an adult, he stood at the rim at last, gazing across a bright blue expanse of water, six miles wide. At 1,932 feet, Crater Lake is the deepest lake in the United States. Steel spent the next seventeen years of his life trying to make the mountain a national park. Using up much of his money, he lectured, lobbied, wrote articles, and circulated petitions. Congress finally responded to his appeals, and Crater Lake National Park was approved in 1902.

Of all the magnificent scenery still without protection as a park at the dawn of the twentieth century, the Grand Canyon of the Colorado River was undoubtedly the most striking. Spanish explorers had seen the canyon in 1540, but the mile-deep gorge had gradually worked its way into the public's consciousness only in the latter half of the 19th century.

In 1857 a U.S. surveying party led by Lt. Joseph Ives traveled up the Colorado River in a steamboat to search for the canyon. Ives finally saw what we now call the Grand Canyon. Although he thought it beautiful, Ives could not imagine anyone else would want to come there. In his report to the government, he wrote: "Ours has been the first, and will doubtless be the last, party of whites to visit this profitless locality." Seldom has a prediction been so wrong.

Major John Wesley Powell fought in the Union Army during the Civil War and lost an arm. Despite his handicap, his spirit of adventure was very much alive. In 1869 he led an expedition down the Colorado River and through the Grand Canyon. The trip by Powell and his men in their wooden boats was the last great journey of exploration in the United States (aside from Alaska). It took the men two months just to travel from southern Wyoming, through Utah, to the eastern edge of the canyon in Arizona.

As they looked ahead and saw the walls of the abyss rising many thousands of feet, the men were worried. So far as they knew, no one had ever traveled through the canyon before. Their only food was bread, bacon, dried fruit, and coffee. The temperature was as high as 115°F. In an entry in his book, dated August 13, Powell wrote: "We are now ready to start on our way down the Great Unknown...We are three quarters of a mile in the depths of the earth, and the great river shrinks into insignificance, as it dashes its angry waves against the walls and cliffs, that rise to the world above...We have an unknown distance yet to run; an unknown river yet to explore."

Nine men entered the canyon that day. But three soon decided that the rapids were too difficult. Deciding to give up the trip, the three climbed to the rim of the canyon—and were quickly killed by Indians. Powell led the rest of his men safely through the canyon, which proved to be more than 200 miles long.

In 1903, President Theodore Roosevelt, a strong supporter of parks, stood at the rim of the canyon. "Do nothing to mar its grandeur," he advised others, "...keep it for your children, your children's children, and all who come after you, as the one great sight which every American should see." But even the Grand Canyon had a rocky path to preservation. Tourists taking Roosevelt's advice flocked to the Arizona Territory to see it. The Santa Fe Railroad completed a spur line to the South Rim, and the grand El Tovar Hotel was erected. The canyon was designated a national monument in 1908, but mining interests fought park status and other men dreamed of building dams and irrigation projects utilizing the rushing waters of the Colorado. Congress finally approved a park bill for the Grand Canyon in 1919, but only after including assurances that existing land claims would not be affected and that power and reclamation projects could be approved by the Secretary of the Interior.

The American Southwest contains thousands of cliff dwellings and other sites where Native Americans lived long ago. As more and more modern-day Americans moved into the Southwest, vandalism and looting of these sites became a problem. Bowls and jewelry and other items could be resold to collectors, and greedy pothunters dug through the ruins. At the Cliff Palace, on Mesa Verde in southwestern Colorado, looters knocked down a wall with blasting powder.

Congress responded in 1906. First, Mesa Verde was made a national park. Second, the Antiquities Act, prohibiting individuals from damaging or removing any historic object from public lands, was signed into law. The act also permitted the president to create, by proclamation, "national monuments." This designation was to be used primarily to protect ancient sites. However, presidents have also proclaimed various forts, battlefields, canyons, and caves as national monuments. The Antiquities Act greatly increased the number of units in the park system, because the monuments did not require the approval of Congress. The prehistoric and historic units of the National Park System are discussed in greater detail in *Historic Monuments of America*, the companion volume to this book.

Devils Tower, in Wyoming, was the first national monument proclaimed by President Roosevelt in 1906. This volcanic rock, resembling the stump of a tree, rises 867 feet above the plains. Most Americans would recognize Devils Tower as the spot where the alien spaceship landed in the motion picture *Close Encounters of the Third Kind*.

Lassen Peak, a volcanic mountain in northern California, was proclaimed a national monument in 1907. The volcano was thought to be extinct, but the experts were wrong! It began to erupt in 1914, and Congress wasted no time in upgrading Lassen to the status of a national park. At about the same time (1912), a powerful volcanic eruption dramatically altered the landscape in the Mount Katmai region in Alaska, and ultimately resulted (1980) in the creation of Katmai National Park and Preserve.

Although the story of the parks is one of continual growth in the amount of acreage given protection, there have been painful setbacks.

Early in the 20th century a lovely part of Yosemite National Park was lost. The city of San Francisco promoted a plan to dam Hetch Hetchy Valley within the park in order to create a lake to augment its water supply. Outraged, John Muir, Yosemite's leading defender, organized a national outcry, arguing that Hetch Hetchy Valley was comparable in beauty to nearby Yosemite Valley.

But the last-ditch effort was doomed to defeat. Congress approved the dam in 1913, and a disheartened John Muir died shortly thereafter. Nonetheless, the cloud of defeat had a silver lining. This dispute was the first major confrontation between the budding conservation movement and Congress. Many individuals who had followed the debate concluded that it was important to protect the parks from any further damage.

By 1916 there were 14 national parks and 21 national monuments. In that year Congress approved the National Parks Organic Act, which stated that the purpose of the parks and monuments was "to conserve the scenery and the natural and historic objects and the wild life therein and…leave them unimpaired for the enjoyment of future generations." Toward that end, the law established a new agency, the National Park Service, to administer the newly designated National Park System.

Stephen T. Mather, a California businessman, had previously written Secretary of the Interior Franklin Lane to complain that the parks were in bad shape. Cattle were grazing inside the parks, and loggers were eager to cut some tall trees that were supposedly protected. Lane wrote back, "Dear Steve: If you don't like the way the national parks are run, why don't you come down to Washington and run them yourself?"

Mather accepted the challenge, becoming the first director of the National Park Service. He had the ability to motivate idealistic young people who wanted to work in the outdoors and do their part to preserve America's natural heritage. He established a tradition of dedication and commitment to the parks that continues to this day.

Mather, by the way, began with a total Park Service administrative budget of $19,500 a year, which included his own salary of $4,500.

Around the same time, concerned parks supporters founded the National Parks and Conservation Association in an effort to "defend the National Parks and Monuments fearlessly against assaults of private interests and aggressive commercialism."

That conditions were poor in the national parks no one could dispute. On the day that Horace Albright, Mather's assistant, inspected a shabby campground in Yellowstone run by fast-buck operators, 20 people were stricken with ptomaine poisoning.

During World War I the fledgling Park Service beat back proposals by food processors to slaughter buffalo and elk in Yellowstone. The processors had contended that the meat was needed for the war effort. In the noble cause of helping to make the world safe for democracy, a few sheep and cattle were allowed to munch on the wildflowers in two parks. During the war the Park Service persuaded Congress to remove the Army from Yellowstone and give the NPS the opportunity to run the park with its own team of rangers. The era of the men and women in the green hats—so familiar and so admired now by millions of visitors—was now underway.

After the war the Park Service could look ahead to a period of rather rapid growth in the number of parks and monuments. The advent of the automobile, driven by tourists with more free time, foreshadowed a sharp increase in the popularity of the parks.

The national parks created so far were all west of the Mississippi River. Glacier and Rocky Mountain National Parks now crowned the crest of the continent, and Hawaii and Alaska each had a park. Most of the parks were of the "monumental" model, and all had been carved from the public domain. But the future would bring parks in the East, some of them smaller in size, some barely snatched from the encroachment of humanity, and some purchased with private or public funds.

In 1919 Lafayette (now Acadia) National Park in Maine became the first park east of the Mississippi River. Undertaking another one-man crusade that lasted for decades, George B. Dorr, a Bostonian and heir to a textile fortune, persuaded his wealthy neighbors on Mount Desert Island to donate land for the park. John D. Rockefeller, Jr. contributed 11,000 acres, almost a third of the park. On the island, granite mountains rise from the sea and overlook a rugged rocky shore that is pounded con-

stantly by the waves of the Atlantic Ocean. Acadia is a dramatic example of nature in conflict with itself.

Other gifts of land or money helped create more parks. In 1926 Great Smoky Mountains (Tennessee, North Carolina), Shenandoah (Virginia), and Mammoth Cave (Kentucky) joined the honor roll. John D. Rockefeller, Jr. again came to the rescue, giving $5 million to the government to buy land for the park in the Smokies. But thousands of average citizens also made donations. Schoolchildren collected pocket change to help save what was left of this virgin forest from the blade of the woodsman's saw. The wisdom of establishing parks in the populous East has been demonstrated many times; the Smokies and Acadia attract far more visitors than either Yellowstone or Yosemite.

Florida's Everglades National Park, authorized in 1934, represented another new departure. This vast "river of grass"—derided by some as an ugly swamp—did not have the visual appeal of snow-capped mountains or green forests, but it did have the East's largest concentration of birds, including masses of graceful egrets, herons, and storks. The park, which also harbors alligators and crocodiles within its mudflats and ponds, was the first to be established primarily because of its wildlife resources.

Rockefeller, meanwhile, was the prime mover in the rescue of another sumptuous landscape. The Grand Tetons of Wyoming, viewed from the sagebrush flats to the east, are perhaps the most sublime mountain façade in the Rockies. They lie within the public domain, and the creation of a small Grand Teton National Park in 1926, limited mostly to the mountains themselves, was no problem. What sends their scenic index off the charts is Jackson Hole, the capacious, open valley of the meandering Snake River, which lies at the base of the 13,000-foot spires. By the 1920s the valley was being checkerboarded with gas stations and billboards. Horace Albright, superintendent at Yellowstone, escorted Rockefeller to Jackson Hole in 1926, and chose a vantage point that required the multimillionaire to peer at the enchanted mountains through a cluster of telephone poles. Rockefeller, though no stranger to private enterprise, was offended by the old dance hall, dilapidated cabins, and other entrepreneurial detritus that spoiled his view. He subsequently agreed to organize the Snake River Land Company, with his own name carefully kept secret (to prevent speculators from driving up prices), and it proceeded to buy up private land in Jackson Hole. By 1933 Rockefeller had spent $1.4 million for 35,000 acres.

When the truth came out, local ranchers and home-steaders, hard hit by the Great Depression, were embittered by the infusion of East Coast wealth to buy their valley. Wyoming political leaders fought for years to prevent the transfer of Rockefeller's purchases for an expanded park. Finally, in 1950, 24 years after committing his resources to a grander Grand Teton Park, Rockefeller could celebrate the addition of Jackson Hole—or most of it—to the park.

The World War II years were quiet ones in the parks, but postwar prosperity brought a new rush of tourists. With the passing decades, visitors had an ever-growing menu of landscapes and seascapes on which to feast their eyes. In Washington state, Mount Olympus and its attendant dripping forests and surf-flogged seashore had become a national park. The haunting cry of a loon at night on a Minnesota lake was preserved for posterity at Voyageurs National Park. The Kodachrome canyon country of southern and eastern Utah, endless twisting avenues of red, white, pink, and orange rock, now contained no fewer than five national parks. Joshua Tree, Saguaro, and Organ Pipe Cactus national monuments protected bizarre plants and ecosystems that only the low hot desert seemed able to harbor.

With the growth of the park system came growing pains. In the 1950s the dam builders and the environmental movement squared off for a second time. Early in the century public protests had failed to prevent the construction of a reservoir in Hetch Hetchy Valley inside Yosemite National Park. Now, the Federal government had its eye on a little known (to the general public) region in the upper drainage of the Colorado River.

Dinosaur National Monument, straddling Utah and Colorado, contains an awesome collection of dinosaur bones. The spines, legbones, and neckbones of the huge reptiles had piled up on a sandbar of a river millions of years ago. Erosion of the land has revealed the bones.

The monument also includes deep canyons of the Green and Yampa rivers. Ever on the lookout for new sources for hydropower, the U.S. Bureau of Reclamation, another agency within the Interior Department, proposed to build a dam at Echo Park, inside the monument.

By this time, however, the environmental movement was much bigger—and better prepared, too.

David Brower, executive director of the Sierra Club, testified that assertions made on behalf of the dam were incorrect. Through the use of scientific studies, Brower demonstrated that the high evaporation rate of the impounded water would make the dam's construction much more expensive than the government had claimed.

In opposing the bill to build the Echo Park Dam, Senator Paul Douglas of Illinois warned that construction of such a reservoir would help transform the country "into a placid, tepid place, greatly unlike the wild and stirring America which we love and from which we draw inspiration." Ultimately, proponents of the dam abandoned the fight in the face of reason and public pressure. The bill before Congress was revised to exclude the Dinosaur dam.

But even in victory, the environmentalists suffered a defeat. The same bill provided for the flooding of the Glen Canyon on the Colorado River in southern Utah. Although the scenery here was lovely, it had not been added to the National Park System. Glen Canyon, so named by Major Powell in 1869, was a secluded world where birdsongs resonated in vaulted stone chambers, waterfalls tinkled into shadowed plunge pools, and the river itself flowed gently, as if resting before it entered the sturm and drang of the Grand Canyon. The Glen Canyon that challenged Powell's literary talents survives only in the fading inks and dyes of *The Place No One Knew: Glen Canyon on the Colorado*, a book of Eliot Porter's photographs, an elegy for a lost world published by the Sierra Club.

Ironically, Lake Powell, the reservoir created by the dam, did become a part of the park system as Glen Canyon National Recreation Area. Many visitors who plow across the lake in motorboats today find the lake and its setting exhilarating, but they do not know what was drowned beneath the water, and they may have difficulty accepting that the dead waters have backed up underneath Rainbow Bridge, arguably the world's most aesthetically pleasing rock formation—and yet another unit in the park system.

Nonetheless, with the defeat of the attempt to build a dam in Dinosaur National Monument, preservationists could claim that they had established the principle that no dams would deface the parks. Right? Wrong! Another painful lesson had yet to be learned: No victories are ever final! Battles that have been "won" may need to be refought by the next generation. And once a particular battle has been lost—once the outstanding feature of a park has been dammed, paved over, or otherwise damaged—the park almost never can be restored to its original beauty.

The law that made the Grand Canyon a national park

in 1919 contained a clause that left open the possibility that dams could be constructed within the gorge. In 1963 the government announced that two dams would be built in the canyon as part of an even broader plan to overcome the water shortage in the Southwest, where cities like Phoenix and Las Vegas were booming. The dams would flood 146 miles of the Colorado River inside the canyon. Behind the dams, the foaming river that had been carving the gorge for eons of time would fall silent and still.

David Brower of the Sierra Club took out full-page newspaper ads in 1966. One said, in part, "...there is only one simple, incredible issue here: this time it's the Grand Canyon they want to flood. *The Grand Canyon!*" Advocates of the dam argued that the reservoir would hardly be visible from the canyon rims, a mile or more above. Bureau of Reclamation director Floyd Dominy pointed out that visitors could travel easily on the lake to examine the billion-year-old rocks up close. Of course, the lake would eliminate one of the world's supreme wilderness adventures, a float trip through the canyon's many whitewater rapids. Another Sierra Club ad posed this question, "Should we also flood the Sistine Chapel so tourists can get nearer the ceiling?"

Charged by the Internal Revenue Service with attempting "substantially" to influence legislation, the Sierra Club was stripped of its tax-exempt status, tripled its membership in two years, and won its fight. When it came time to twist senatorial arms in Capitol cloakrooms, defenders of the Grand Canyon pointed out that the dams would serve only as cash registers, and that hydroelectric power generated by the dams would be sold to finance the construction of water development elsewhere. Other sources, they demonstrated, could provide electric power at less cost.

A blizzard of letters to Congress denounced the dams. Convinced that they were right and knowing that the public was behind them, the conservationists refused to compromise. Neither dam was built.

In 1961 the U.S. government established a precedent by spending $16 million of the taxpayers' money to purchase the land for Cape Cod National Seashore in Massachusetts. That amount, however, was a pittance compared with the cost for Redwood National Park in California. The coast redwood trees are the world's tallest living things—not to be confused with their woody cousins, the sequoias, in the Sierra Nevada, which are the world's most massive living objects. Through the efforts of John Muir and his disciples, the greatest stands of the Sierran forests had been protected in national parks established in 1890. But the redwoods, flourishing amid the fog and moisture of the northern California coast, were mostly in the possession of logging companies who saw in them fine pieces of furniture. The clearcutting of virgin redwoods accelerated beyond the rate of 1,000,000 board feet per year in the 1950s. The Save-the-Redwoods League, later joined by the Sierra Club, worked tirelessly for decades to save the trees, and the Muir Woods National Monument (1908) and several state parks were established to preserve several parcels of forest.

But a survey released in 1964 showed that 85 percent of the primeval redwoods had already fallen. Congress acted to bring 58,000 acres into a Redwood National Park in 1968 that included a "legislative taking" of private land. Benefits to be paid to loggers who lost their jobs were projected at $100 million, and the overall cost, including the purchase of 48,000 more acres in 1978, approached the $1 billion mark.

In the late 1970s the National Park System comprised about 300 units containing some 30 million acres. But then, the addition of only a few more parks and monuments more than doubled the acreage of the system. Late in the 20th century, this dramatic expansion could have occurred in only one state, Alaska. The nation's largest state, more than twice the size of Texas, Alaska was also by far the wildest and least populated. Relatively few Americans were hardy enough or sufficiently dedicated to accept Alaska on its own harsh terms.

Before statehood (1959) the Federal government owned 99 percent of Alaska, and the state was admitted to the Union with the understanding that it would get 100 million acres (out of a total of 375 million). The native Alaskans—Inuits (Eskimos), Aleuts, and Indians—also asserted claims for land. In 1971, Congress agreed to give the natives 44 million acres and nearly $1 billion. Thanks to the efforts of Dr. Edgar Wayburn of the Sierra Club and many other environmentalists, that law also provided that the government study up to 80 million acres for possible inclusion in the national parks, national forests, and national wildlife refuges. Phenomenally complex negotiations got under way, with the natives and the development-minded state politicians battling with the Federal government over which lands they would control and which lands would go to the parks.

In 1978, with the deadline at hand for Congress to implement the clause in the 1971 law that authorized new parks, and with no agreement in sight, President Jimmy Carter used his authority to create national monuments, thus protecting the scenery-rich landscapes until the final park boundaries could be drawn. That was accomplished in 1980. Ronald Reagan, who was unsympathetic to the preservationists' maximum dreams for Alaskan parklands, had just been elected president. Therefore, in the subsequent lame duck session of Congress preceding Reagan's inauguration, the House settled for a compromise Senate bill that was less protective than the House majority had wanted.

Nonetheless, what additions had been made to the "crown jewels," and what new meaning had been given to that description! Denali National Park was tripled in size to 6,000,000 acres. Its crowning glory, Mount McKinley, the top of the continent, splits the sky 18,000 feet above its base, at an altitude of 20,320 feet. The seashore mountains of Wrangell-St. Elias shrink human contrivances to near-invisibility, and whole states of people could be hidden within the park's 13.2 million empty acres. In Lake Clark National Park and Preserve, smoking volcanoes riding on restless tectonic plates promise more conflict between the forces of fire and ice. The permanently frozen ground and howling wilderness of Gates of the Arctic National Park and Preserve provide the ultimate test of our resourcefulness as matched against the uncaring laws of nature.

Altogether, eight areas in Alaska bear the designation "park" or "park and preserve." The great achievement in Alaska is that entire ecosystems—river basins, mountain ranges—have been preserved. Migration routes of animal herds have been protected. Mistakes made in the allocation of park acreage in the "lower 48" have by and large been avoided in Alaska. If Alaska is the Last Frontier, as its boomers call it, it may also be the last best hope on Earth for survival of what is left of nature's kingdom.

The National Park System of 1990 embraces 354 units, with more than half of them classified as historical. At 0.02 acres, Thaddeus Kosciuszko National Memorial in Philadelphia is the antipode of Wrangell-St. Elias. Some 80 million acres are distributed across 49 states (Delaware is the exception), the District of Columbia, American Samoa, Puerto Rico, the Virgin Islands, Guam, and Saipan. Annual visits exceed 300 million. The units fall into 23 categories, including such fine distinctions as national rivers and national wild and scenic riverways. There is one national mall (in the District of Columbia) and the White House, which is in a classification by itself.

(National forests and national wildlife refuges are not part of the National Park System.)

Superimposed on this jargon jungle is another kind of classification—wilderness. The Wilderness Act of 1964, the goal of The Wilderness Society for a generation, designates areas in the United States where "there shall be no commercial enterprise and no permanent road...no use of motor vehicles, motorized equipment or motor boats, no landing of aircraft, no other form of mechanical transport, and no structure or installation." Those who make a living extracting minerals from the ground or letting livestock graze upon it were aghast at the idea of "locking up" vast tracts of land as wilderness. But proponents did not visualize setting aside more than a small percentage of the American landscape as wilderness. The effect of the Wilderness Act on the parks was that of creating zones, one in which no motorized activity was permitted, and one in which a greater variety of recreation was allowed. Not all the wilderness was to be drawn from National Park Service lands; acreage administered by the U.S. Forest Service, Fish and Wildlife Service, and Bureau of Land Management was also to be considered for such protection.

The process of evaluating and designating wilderness areas continues in 1990, 25 years after the act was adopted, with "special interests" fighting state-by-state to keep the wilderness areas as small in size and in number as possible. But public sentiment continued to run strongly in favor of wilderness. Millions of Americans whose recreational pursuits did not include backpacking and canoeing simply wanted to know that untouched country still existed, perhaps even idyllic places where lions lay down with lambs, and mysterious places populated with water sprites and trolls.

Only a minority of the visitors to the parks are seeking wilderness. On a typical summer weekend, over 50,000 visitors park their campers or pitch their tents in the 450 campgrounds administered by the Park Service. Indeed, the upper portion of Yosemite Valley has long resembled a small town, featuring at one time or another tennis courts, a pitch-and-putt golf course, a bank, a delicatessen, a skating rink, three swimming pools, a barber shop, a beauty shop, thirty-three kennels, and thirteen package liquor stores.

The Park Service went through a period in which somewhat unnatural entertainment was provided for visitors. Both the Yellowstone Act of 1872 and the National Park Service Act of 1916 had said that the parks must not only preserve nature but also provide enjoyment for visitors. Early directors, eager to build rapidly a constituency in support of the national park concept, fostered the entertainment aspect. Grandstands were built at Yellowstone to provide a good view of bears being fed garbage. Other animals were chained near the hotels. Floodlights illuminated Old Faithful at night. In Yosemite Valley, logs and bark were set on fire and pushed off the 3,000-foot Glacier Point at night to thrill visitors. The grandeur of nature was reduced to serving as a source of cheap amusement, and those Yellowstone bears became beggars that sometimes even attacked visitors.

Today, swimming pools and animal exhibitions are out, and the official policy is that animals take precedence over people. There is less human effort to control wildlife populations, and age-old predator-prey relationships are being restored where possible.

As a footnote to all this, it should be noted that the government has received plenty of free advice about how to entertain visitors. In 1923, when the town of Shelby, Montana, had a surplus of natural gas and Glacier National Park had no volcanoes (it still doesn't have any), a plan was floated to pipe the gas sixty miles to Chief Mountain within the park, where it would serve to create eruptions that, according to one article, would "rival Vesuvius or any of the other Old World 'smokers.'"

The most serious threats to the parks are the most subtle ones, and they are revealed in the slow degradation of the park experience. Pollution from power plants and coastal cities has gradually reduced the broad crystal-clear vistas in the open country of the West. In the East, an unnatural, manmade haze mixes with the natural blue haze that gives the Smokies their name. Throughout the country, even in Acadia National Park in Maine, far distant from major population centers, sulfur-laden acid rain is killing forests as well as the inhabitants of ponds and lakes. Streams flowing through parks carry sewage and pesticides that poison wildlife. In the Grand Canyon, wilderness campers and hikers were distracted by the buzzing of 50,000 sightseeing overflights a year by helicopters and small planes, many of which swooped below the canyon rims. It took a mid-air collision of two planes killing 25 people over the canyon in 1986 to spur Congress to reduce the number of overflights. Competing preferences of visitors must be weighed, with a compromise that fails to satisfy anybody the almost certain result.

In its *State of the Parks 1980* report to Congress, the National Park Service declared Glacier National Park to be the most endangered park in the system. The National Parks and Conservation Association, examining the park eight years later, found little improvement. Aside from the usual documented troubles—poaching, livestock wandering onto park land, air pollution, and helicopter overflights—Glacier had special problems, too many of them shared with other parks as well. Clearcutting along park borders constituted not only an eyesore but a threat to wildlife that migrated in and out of the park. Oil companies, searching for oil and gas preserves, detonated explosives right up to the park boundaries, shattering the solitude of wilderness explorers. Prospective mining in Canada would pollute the North Fork of the Flathead River upstream of the park. The suppression of naturally caused fires carried with it the threat of uncontrollable blazes in the future.

The conservationist Aldo Leopold wrote that across the vast prairie of the Midwest the tall grass once tickled the bellies of millions of buffalo. Most of the buffalo are gone, and the same must be said of the bluestem and other grasses that once covered 400,000 square miles. But in Kansas and Oklahoma, fragments of the tallgrass prairie still survive, where the windblown fields roll like ocean waves in a stiff breeze. If the terms of purchase can be worked out, a Tallgrass Prairie National Preserve will join our roster of monuments.

The consideration of other potential future parks, those having national rather than regional significance, continues. No one is likely to discover another Yosemite Valley, but Congress is considering a Mojave National Park in California that would preserve the threatened desert lying within a short jaunt of millions of people. The Big Sur section of the California coastline deserves to be included, and the same holds true for other Anasazi ruins and rock art of the Southwest. The San Rafael Swell, a bizarre broken country of naked sandstone in eastern Utah, must have protection to survive threats from mining and off-road vehicles. The Florida Keys and the Columbia River Gorge cry out for additional protection.

The distinguished writer Wallace Stegner has observed, "No other nation on Earth so swiftly wasted its birthright; no other, in time, made such an effort to save what was left." Perhaps hearing the yet-unspoken pleas of descendants that they would never know, certainly mindful of a nearly defenseless natural world, much of which they would never see, enough Americans came forward to say, "these monuments we must honor." In coming to the rescue of the natural world, man symbolically rejoined it.

The East

In Acadia National Park, along the famous "rockbound coast" of Maine, the sea constantly pounds against the tall cliffs. Thousands of years ago, during the Ice Age, massive glaciers also tore at the granite fortress.

The rocky shoreline, underwater ledges, and deep fog have always been a threat to boats and ships passing near Acadia. The Bass Harbor Head Light has sent out its warning of danger since 1858.

In Shenandoah National Park, in Virginia, waterfalls like this one in White Oak Canyon drop sharply from the Blue Ridge, which forms the eastern rampart of the Appalachian Mountains. The Skyline Drive follows the length of the ridge throughout the park.

In the continental United States the day begins in Maine, and in Acadia National Park it very often emerges from a seamless white fog. Yielding to the burning power of a rising but yet unseen sun, the fog draws back slowly, affording a wondrous sight, conjuring before your eyes the Creation of Genesis. From where you stand an ever-broader and sloping shelf of boulders—jagged, slippery, aimlessly tossed yet curiously sorted by size, and strewn with kelp—comes into view.

Beyond the "rockbound coast" you can now see an ever-larger expanse of water, not alive yet never still, heedless of time yet synchronized precisely with movements of the sun and moon, allowing calculations of the tides to the minute. Up from the beach, the parting mists reveal scrubby vegetation surrounding a quiet lily pond occupied by waterfowl. Finally, in the east, a strange pale sun appears, generating light but no heat, above an assumed horizon in a still-invisible sky. Perhaps only by mid-morning is a conventional world fully in place, warm, vast in scale, under a blue bowl painted with soaring gulls, and bordered by carpets of conifers thrown over granite mountains.

Acadia occupies most of Mount Desert Island, which was largely formed hundreds of millions of years ago by the upwelling of magma from deep in the earth, then scoured by glaciers within the past eighteen thousand years. Today another force, the Atlantic Ocean, tears at the stone fortress. From the peak of Cadillac Mountain, 1,530 feet, highest on the eastern seaboard, one can see

The Appalachian Mountains, which are very old, rounded, and worn down from their original height, reach to the horizon, range after range, from Shenandoah National Park.

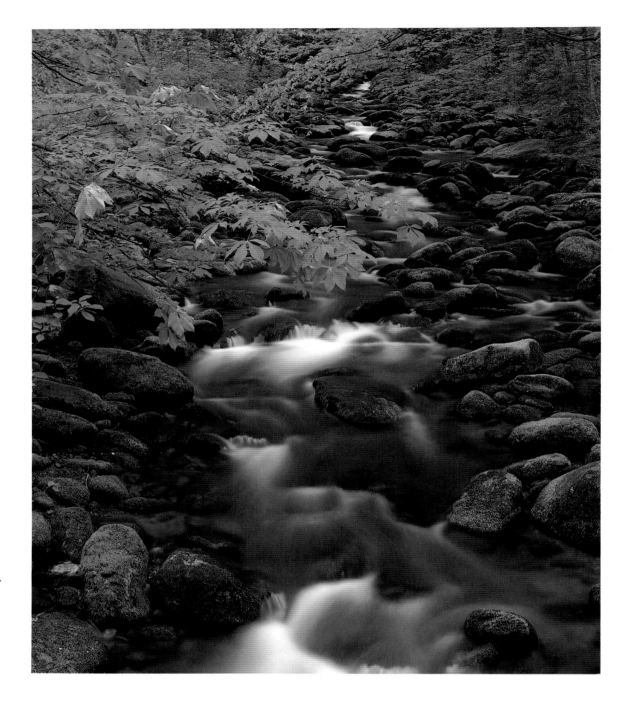

Heavy rain and snowfall in Great Smoky Mountains National Park send cascades of water spilling in every direction. The precipitation and the fertile soil have produced one of the world's richest collections of trees and other plants outside the tropics.

islands that were part of the mainland until the ocean, rising with melted ice, surrounded them.

Along the coast, in the intertidal zones exposed only at low or intermediate tides, many plants and animals flourish in spite of assaults of the sea. Marine snails called periwinkles graze on the blue-green alga, which has stained the rocks black. Millions of acorn barnacles cling to the rocks. The rubbery rockweed, anchored to the rocks by tentacles called holdfasts, lies prostrate when exposed but floats upright when underwater. Further down, in zones exposed only rarely during low tides, crabs, sea stars, and sea urchins settle in among the Irish moss and kelp. At sea, porpoises, seals, and five species of whales consume fish, squid, and other ocean creatures.

With all the scattered villages and inholdings, Mount Desert Island and the park are less than a wilderness. But the cycle of nature, first forceful, then serene, is dominant.

Some 120 miles northwest of Acadia, Mount Katahdin rises 5,267 feet above the lay of the land, the highest point in Maine, the centerpiece of Baxter State Park, and northern terminus for the 2,100-mile Appalachian National Scenic Trail. Constructed by volunteers from 1922 to 1927, the trail

The sun sets beyond the hazy mountains that give the Great Smokies their name. Hydrocarbons and water vapor released by plant life creates the haze.

Establishment of a park in the Great Smoky Mountains in the 1920s prevented further logging of the finest forest in the eastern United States. Millions of people contributed money to help purchase the land for the park.

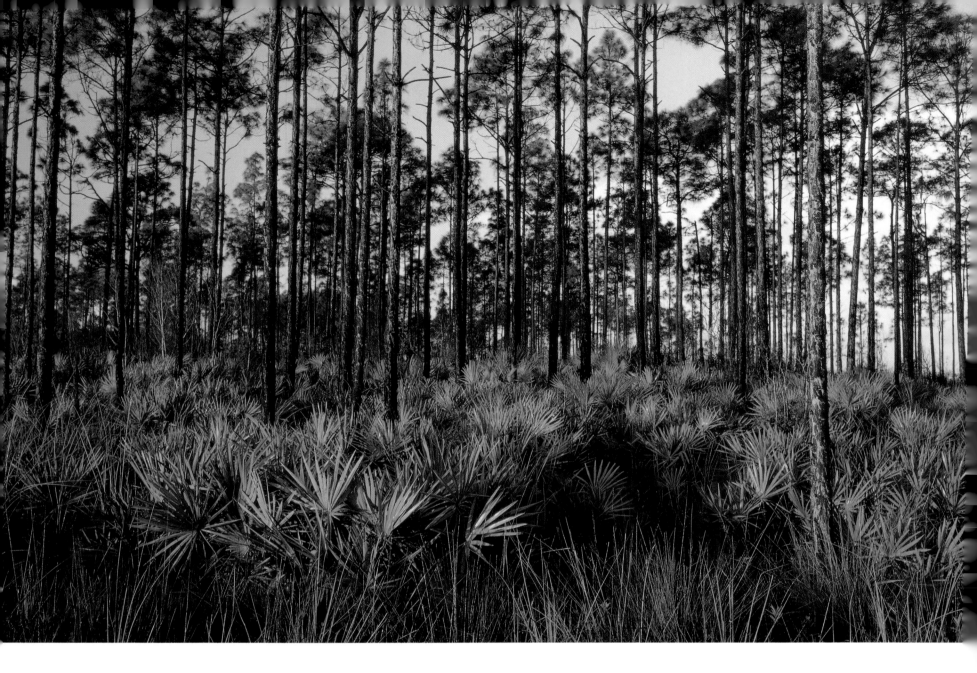

In the broad flat expanse of Everglades National Park, the slash pines shown here flourish because their thick corky bark resists the fires that often break out. Palmettos grow beneath the pines.

has welcomed uncounted thousands of visitors who have hiked a portion of it, as well as an energetic few who have walked its entire length.

For those who attempt the entire distance at one time, months are required, and the usual approach is to begin in April at the southern terminus, Springer Mountain in Georgia, and follow the changing seasons north. Through fourteen states, the trail follows the dominant topographic feature of the East, the Appalachian Mountains—really a nearly continuous chain of ranges, including the Great Smokies, the Blue Ridge, Lehigh and South mountains, the Catskills, and the Taconic, White, and Green mountains of New England. As mountains go, the Appalachians are quite old, and erosion—the great leveller—has worn down and rounded off the system's numberless peaks.

Rich in coal, iron ore, marble, and granite, Appalachia is nonetheless the home of too many impoverished people, abandoned along with emptied quarries and strip-mined land when corporations and other entrepreneurs moved their operations elsewhere. Tourism has brought a lift to some parts of the mountain region, as millions of residents of the crowded East seek refuge in the state and Federal recreation areas in the high country, including Great Smoky Mountains and Shenandoah national parks. The Appalachian Trail meanders through these parks, but far more Americans gain access to them through a paved trail more suited to four wheels than two feet.

The town of Front Royal, Virginia, in an apple-growing region sixty miles west of Washington, D.C., is the jumping-off place for perhaps the longest automobile odyssey in the park system, and one of the most appealing. Just south of Front Royal, a left turn brings motorists onto Skyline Drive and into Shenandoah National Park. For 105 miles to the southwest through the pencil-shaped park, the drive follows the crest of the range. (Contrary to the song's lyrics—"In the Blue Ridge Mountains of Virginia/On the trail of the lonesome pine"—it's just the Blue Ridge.) The Skyline Drive is so famous in itself that many people traverse it without realizing that they are also in a park called Shenandoah.

The Blue Ridge here forms the eastern rampart of the Appalachians. The metamorphic and igneous rock is as much as one billion years old; to the west, the looping Shenandoah River is visible for the length of the park. South of where the river splits into its northern and southern forks, the 40-mile-long Massanutten Mountain rises within the valley itself.

In 1926, by the time the park was authorized, many settlers on the ridge had migrated elsewhere in search of a better living, and the government subsequently bought out or resettled the rest. A forest of oak, hickory, and a hundred other species now spreads across 95 percent of the park, and indeed two-fifths of the park has been designated a wilderness by Congress. Deer, bears, bobcats, and turkeys, once missing or rare, have returned. Trails lead steeply down the sides of the ridge, alive in the spring with banks of pink azaleas and mountain laurel and cascades of water. Fall foliage is brilliant, and open winter vistas from the ridge lift the spirits.

The highway, after dropping into Rockfish Gap near Waynesboro, exits the park and metamor-

Pine Glades Lake in Everglades National Park. Water moves through the park in a most unusual river that is 50 miles wide and only six inches deep.

Alligators, which are common in the Everglades, conserve energy by resting motionless most of the time, and they may take a meal only once or twice a week. The heron in the foreground is a potential meal.

Great egrets gather in the early morning at Mrazek Pond in the Everglades. These wading birds hunt for food in shallow water. Fish, frogs, and snakes are all on their menu.

phoses into the Blue Ridge Parkway, a unit in the National Park System by that name. For 469 miles, in Virginia and North Carolina, the road passes along some of the grandest mountain scenery in the eastern United States at an average altitude of 3,000 feet. Turnouts provide panorama after panorama of craggy mountains and haze-dimmed valleys.

The rusticity of the Blue Ridge is tied a great deal to the preserved homesteads of the old-timers who once lived here, operating moonshine stills and all too often communicating with their neighbors through exchanges of shotgun blasts. Split rail fences, log cabins, and old gristmills are part of the charm of the Blue Ridge country. Mount Mitchell, the highest mountain east of the Mississippi River at an elevation of 6,684 feet, rises just to the west of the parkway in North Carolina.

The parkway terminates at the southern entrance to Great Smoky Mountains National Park. The Smokies are the culmination of the Southern Appalachians, and from vantage points they roll away to the horizon, tier after tier.

Clouds moving in from the west are pushed up by the mountains and release their moisture. Into each life, it is said, some rain must fall, and the prolific life of the Smokies relies on a great deal of precipitation, which can be snowflakes in the highlands and drizzle in the lowlands, simultaneously. Fog smothers the forest in the morning, and the sight and sound of numerous cascades and swift streams add to the pervasive sense of dampness.

The precipitation and the fertile soils have created a world-renowned flora—1,400 kinds of flowering plants, 130 trees, 230 lichens, almost 300 mosses and liverworts, and at least 2,000 fungi. Trees are everywhere, blanketing almost the entire park. Higher elevations feature the red spruce more familiar to Maine and. Canada. Beeches, maples, birches, and buckeyes occupy the middle slope—a visual treat in autumn. The southern hardwood forests are loveliest in spring, when flowering dogwoods and silver bells blossom.

Red, white, and pink rhododendrons crowd the summits and slopes in summer while trillium, spring beauties, bluets, and trout lilies flood the forest floor in the spring. This great mass of plant life, rarely equaled in temperate zones worldwide, exudes the hydrocarbons and water vapor that form the highlands' filmy haze, or "smoke."

The most frequently encountered representative of the animal kingdom is *Homo sapiens*, and more than 8,000,000 of them can be seen in the park each year. Indeed, the Great Smokies is the park most often visited by this species. Because the woods are so dense, and because many human visitors stay inside or near their metal carapaces, they can easily be avoided by hikers who venture onto the 900 miles of trails. In the woods, with luck, black bears may even be sighted more frequently. Bears have the good sense to sleep through the winter, and hairless eight-ounce cubs, usually two in number, are born in January while mother dozes away, often in a hollow high on a tree. By March, the furred cubs and their mother are ready to join, or rejoin, the world.

Water, in the form of precipitation, creates the beauty of the Great Smokies, and direct interactions between land and water are responsible for other unique and protected environments of the East.

Everglades National Park, at the southern tip of the Florida mainland, is the largest eastern park, but it may not be large enough to survive, and indeed Everglades may become an extinct park as

Fish of many colors, including the parrotfish (front center) and banded butterfly fish (front right) swim among the fascinating coral formations of Buck Island Reef National Monument in the Caribbean.

the natural systems outside and within the preserve decline to the point where the park can no longer sustain its resident wildlife. The park cannot be described or discussed in isolation from the fact of its decline.

The Everglades has been called a river of grass, but the river is most unusual, six inches deep, 50 miles wide, 100 miles long. Water advances generally southward toward the Bay of Florida in a broad shallow sheet at the rate of one-half mile per day, on a gradient of two or three inches per mile. The river is underlain with limestone, which supports the sawgrass that occupies it. The land is so flat that the highest points of ground—one at an elevation of twenty feet—are piles of shells discarded by the indigenous peoples of many centuries ago. Islands called hammocks rise one to three feet above the limestone and support hardwoods that include live oak, mahogany, and strangler fig. Thick stands of mangroves crowd the coast, where salt water and fresh water mix.

This, the largest subtropical wilderness in the contiguous states, is home to alligators, crocodiles, panthers, and a world-renowned assemblage of wading birds. But no more than thirty panthers survive in the "Glades" and in the Big Cypress Preserve to the north. Crocodiles are rare, too. The waders have declined by 90 percent since the 1930s, though they still gather in impressive numbers in drying pools in winter to harvest fish, frogs, and other edible creatures.

The boom in human population in South Florida has placed a heavy strain on the water supply and on other species that depend on its unobstructed movement. The watershed for the Everglades is 240 miles to the north. But in the 1940s the U.S. Army Corps of Engineers began to channelize

The white-sand beaches of Virgin Islands National Park, on the island of St. John, consist of particles of coral ground to bits by heavy storms. This is Cinnamon Bay.

Horn Island, in Gulf Islands National Seashore, is off the coast of Mississippi. These barrier islands, which are wildlife sanctuaries, buffer the mainland from the destructive force of violent ocean-borne storms.

the Kissimmee River and send its flow into Lake Okeechobee. In turn that water was removed from the lake, to supply the needs of agriculture as well as Miami and other cities, by means of a complex of canals, dikes, and levees. The supply of water to the Everglades fell sharply. As the fish declined in number, wading birds stopped nesting. Rather than see their young starve, for example, resident wood storks declined to nest for several consecutive years in the 1980s.

Even the gentle manatees, or sea cows, that swim the waters of Florida Bay are being thinned by bloody encounters with the propellers of motorboats.

Many Floridians are working tirelessly to prevent the demise of the park, by prevailing on the U.S. government to restore the Kissimmee River to its natural state and add more acreage to the park. But time may not be on their side.

Twenty-one miles east of Everglades, in Florida's "other" park, the news is better. Biscayne National Park, 95 percent underwater, occupies a short strip of mangrove-choked mainland, most of Biscayne Bay, a string of over 40 low islands, or keys, and a stretch of open sea. Early in the century pollutants were poisoning the portion of Biscayne Bay nearest to Miami, but the bay is recovering well. Indeed, the southern section is nearly pristine.

Biscayne is for snorkelers who swim past the coral reefs, underground rock fortresses up to 100 feet high. The reefs are the work of millions of small animals called polyps, who have the magical ability to take chemicals from the sea and convert them to stone. As the polyps harden and be-

Heron, Padre Islands National Seashore, Texas. This wildlife sanctuary on the Gulf of Mexico includes 80 miles of white sand-and-shell beaches, dunes, grasslands, and tidal flats teeming with shore birds.

Cape Hatteras National Seashore includes barrier islands off the North Carolina mainland that absorb the full force of ocean storms. Since 1870 this lighthouse has sent out its illuminated warning to ships passing through the so-called Graveyard of the Atlantic.

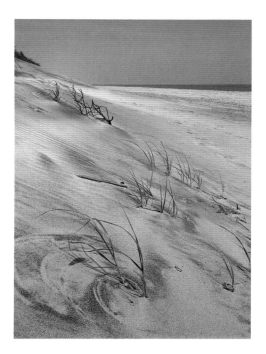

Fire Island National Seashore, off the coast of Long Island, contains the first designated wilderness area in New York State, and is easily accessible to millions of people living in New York City and its suburbs.

come a permanent part of the reef, new generations grow atop the old. Nature's wildest indulgences are displayed here. Corals may take the form of deer antlers or the corrugated surface of the human brain.

And among the reefs swim fish of brilliant iridescent colors. Many move in schools, but the queen angelfish, an intense blue and yellow, passes with deliberate grace. In waters where pirates once prowled, the most sinister inhabitants today are octopuses, eels, hammerhead sharks, and stingrays.

Water is also the catalyst for America's tropical paradise, the Caribbean island of St. John in the U.S. Virgin Islands. Virgin Islands National Park, though small as parks go, is rich in species of plant and animal life. Born of volcanic action, the home long ago of warlike Carib Indians and later of Danish sugar plantation masters and their black slaves, the islands today show little evidence of their tempestuous past. The forest of St. John, once leveled to make room for sugar cane and cotton, has regrown and, if not precisely of its original composition, it is sufficiently jungle-like to suit backcountry hikers.

If Columbus, who discovered the islands in 1493 and named them for St. Ursula and her 11,000 virgins, were to return today, he would still find quiet coves, limpid blue-green waters, and white sandy beaches fringed by lush green hills. In the low dry southeastern part of St. John, cactus and other desert plants replace the dense growth of the higher elevations.

Bats, the only native mammals, scoop bothersome insects out of the air. Mongooses, donkeys, and goats, all introduced species, eat some park resources. Lizards are everywhere. Geckos, snakes, and iguanas may cross your trail, not to mention an army of hermit crabs moving through the uplands. The abundant bird life ranges from pelicans to hummingbirds and cuckoos. The white beaches—Trunk Bay's is considered one of the world's ten best—are formed from particles of hard coral, smashed to bits by storm-tossed waves. Snorkelers can hear parrotfish chewing on the reef and grunts grunting, and can swim past the curious trunkfish as it spits a stream of water into the sand to uncover prey.

Buck Island Reef National Monument, 1.5 miles from St. Croix, largest of the Virgin Islands, is another destination for snorkelers. Frigate birds glide for hours, riding the currents over the island

Ponies roam wild on Assateague Island, part of which is included in a national seashore. In this marshland, stretching along the Atlantic coast between Virginia and Maryland, ponies such as these are used to getting their feet wet!

Autumn is a time of special beauty at the Delaware Water Gap National Recreation Area, where the Delaware River, which divides New Jersey and Pennsylvania, has cut through the Appalachian Mountains.

and its submerged reef teeming with marine life.

Along the eastern seaboard of the U.S. mainland, at the interface between ocean and land, seven national seashores preserve fragments of the coast as it (approximately) was at the time seafaring explorers and the first early settlers sailed past in the 1600s.

Most of the seashores are barrier islands, long strips of sand paralleling the mainland, and they take a fierce pounding from both nature and man. Many of the eastern barrier islands have been developed and are inaccessible to the public. Storms and occasional hurricanes flog the beaches, rearranging the sand dunes and damaging or even destroying property, often astonishing vacation-home owners who, one gathers, were naive enough to buy land on the basis of slick brochures with picture-postcard views of serene and sunny seascapes. But the Atlantic is not a pacific ocean, and when nature bestirs itself we can be instructed on its fury and caprice. Most of the Outer Banks of North Carolina are now part of Cape Hatteras and Cape Lookout national seashores. The treacherous waters off the coast of the Outer Banks—the Graveyard of the Atlantic—and a few German submarines have claimed more than 600 ships. Storms sometimes uncover the ruins of old wrecks buried on the beaches.

The eastern beaches must also endure water polluted by medical waste, oil spills, and garbage discharged from ships. Offshore oil and gas development is a threat, and off-road vehicles chew up

Pictured Rocks National Lakeshore, along the edge of Lake Superior in Michigan, features a wall of rock that has been sculptured into caves, arches, and formations resembling castles and fortresses.

the dunes and obliterate fragile plants that help anchor the sand.

America's four national lakeshores are all found along the shores of the Great Lakes. These are gentler places as a rule, though towering dunes of glacial till and scoured bedrock are reminders of the force with which glaciers carved the lakes thousands of years ago.

The lake country is also home to two national parks. Isle Royale National Park occupies an island 45 miles long and nine miles wide in Lake Superior. The park, 99 percent wilderness, contains 166 miles of hiking trails and zero miles of highway, and access is by boat and float plane only. Visibly, dramatically scraped by glaciers of immense weight, the island's volcanic rock slowly emerged as the level of the lake fell. Soil then developed, and plants and animals moved in. Today, the deep forests and small inland lakes provide one of the most secluded wilderness experiences in the contiguous states. In a recent year, only 13,000 visits were recorded on Isle Royale, the largest island in the largest freshwater lake in the world.

Moose swam to the island from Canada early in the century and proceeded to consume all of their food supply. Their numbers crashed, then recovered after a 1936 fire cleared the way for the regrowth of "moose salad." Eastern timber wolves crossed from the mainland on an ice bridge in 1948-1949, and proceeded to do the moose the considerable favor of culling their ranks of the old and ill. The rest of the moose stayed within their food supply and flourished. Sooner or later, however, it is the fate of almost every moose to perish in an assault by one of the highly organized and disciplined wolfpacks. Biologists have studied the wolf-moose relationship since 1958, and several books and many reports and articles have been the result. The numbers of predator and prey continue to rise and fall in relationship to each other.

One of Minnesota's nicknames is The Land of Ten Thousand Lakes, and 30 of them are within Voyageurs National Park along the Canadian border. Four times within the last million years—and as recently as 11,000 years ago—massive ice sheets up to two miles in depth scraped across this

Cape Cod was created thousands of years ago when glaciers pushed across New England and piled up debris to form the peninsula that now rises above the sea. Cape Cod National Seashore contains beaches, dunes, freshwater ponds, woodlands, and marshes.

Sleeping Bear Dunes National Lakeshore, on the northwestern shore of Michigan's lower peninsula, is a hilly region replete with small lakes, massive coastal sand dunes, and rugged bluffs rising as high as 460 feet above Lake Michigan.

Twenty-one islands in Lake Superior and a portion of Bayfield Peninsula comprise Apostle Islands National Lakeshore in Wisconsin. Lake Superior is the largest body of fresh water in the world.

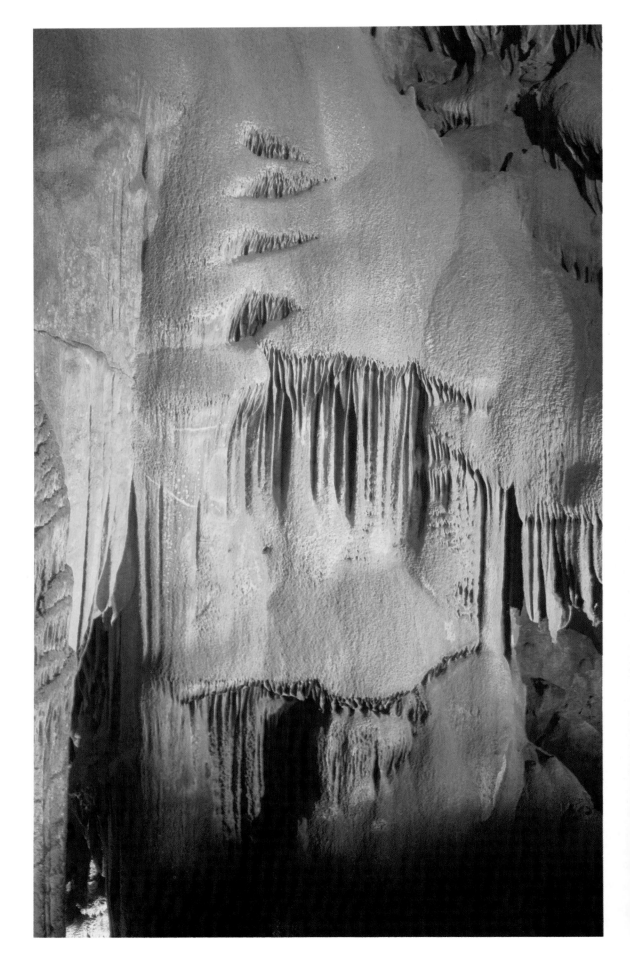

The world's longest cave system, with 330 miles of passageways discovered so far, winds underneath the ground in Kentucky. Mammoth Cave National Park includes a river and forest above ground, as well as the limestone cavern, which features this formation called Frozen Niagara.

land, erasing part of the geologic record and deeply furrowing what was left. Some of the world's oldest rock, up to 2.7 billion years old, has been exposed within the park.

Voyageurs was named for the French-Canadian canoeists who transported beaver and other pelts between Montreal and the Canadian Northwest by birchbark canoe in the late 18th and early 19th centuries. Today, roads lead only to the edges of the park, and canoes and other boats are the chief form of travel. In winter, cross-country skiing and snowmobiling are options. The howl of the wolf and the cry of the loon on a moonlit night are worth whatever trouble it took to reach this remote land of forest and water.

Mammoth Cave, in Kentucky, contains more than 330 miles of passageway explored and mapped so far, making this by far the longest known cave system in the world. According to legend, the entrance to Mammoth Cave was discovered in 1797 by a hunter who was chasing a bear, or vice versa. The cave soon became a tourist attraction, one of the first in the United States. Stephen Bishop, a self-educated slave who was an early guide, gained a measure of fame beginning in the 1830s as he discovered more than twenty miles of passageway.

The cave has been dissolved out of limestone beds deposited more than 300 million years ago. Uplift of the land cracked the limestone, and water, working its way toward the nearby Green River, percolated through the cracks and gradually widened them. This sculpturing has produced immense interior spaces, including the 192-foot-high Mammoth Dome and the 105-foot-deep Bottomless Pit. Rivers flow far underground. Sparkling white gypsum crystals, stalactites, and stalagmites are among the decorations.

In a world of perpetual darkness, eyes are useless, and blind creatures have evolved, including fish, spiders, daddy longlegs, and beetles. The cave critters survive in part on dung dropped in the cave by bats and crickets paying visits from the world of light.

Voyageurs National Park in northern Minnesota is a wilderness park, and canoes and other small vessels provide the only easy access to this region of seemingly numberless islands, lakes, and bays.

The North Woods in Voyageurs National Park contains many birch trees, which provided the source for construction of the birch-bark canoes that the early French-Canadian voyageurs used to transport furs across the lakes region.

Plains and Mountains

In Montana's Glacier National Park, water in Avalanche Creek flows swiftly off a high-mountain glacier. Glacier borders a Canadian park and thus also represents the U.S. portion of Waterton-Glacier International Peace Park.

Volcanic ash and other sediments that have solidified constitute the surface of the land in Badlands National Park in South Dakota. Rain, though infrequent, tears at the soft strata and produces jagged ridges, steep canyons, gullies, and spires.

This rugged, dry landscape is in Theodore Roosevelt National Park, which honors our 26th president. Roosevelt, who owned a ranch in the area, was a strong advocate for national parks, monuments, and wildlife refuges.

Almost imperceptibly, the Great Plains slope downward from the base of the Rocky Mountains, falling from an altitude of 6,000 feet in Colorado and Wyoming to about 1,000 feet on merging with the Mississippi Valley. Across 400 miles from west to east, the decline is barely ten feet per mile. Buffalo no longer roam free by the millions nibbling native grasses, which have yielded to corn and wheat. Winds still blow and tumbleweeds still tumble, though now the terrain is laced with many fences. The Dust Bowl of the 1930s remains a warning to those who seek to cultivate the land without regard to the rules of nature.

Theodore Roosevelt, looking very much the innocent eastern dude, first traveled from his home in New York to the plains in the Dakota Territory in 1883. The bespectacled Harvard graduate took an unlikely interest in running a cattle ranch. After being devastated by the deaths of his wife and mother on the same day in 1884, Roosevelt returned to Dakota, to the town of Medora, and bought into one ranch and started building another. Soon he was running 4,500 head of cattle. The future president also hoped to hunt buffalo, but the wild herds had been virtually wiped out. "TR" was dismayed by the uncontrolled overgrazing that had destroyed the grasslands and reduced habitat for songbirds and small mammals. He eventually channeled most of his energies elsewhere, and sold out in 1898 before dashing off to Cuba to lead his Rough Riders from the plains in the Spanish-American War.

Roosevelt left the cattle country as a conservationist who later wrote, "I never would have been President if it had not been for my experiences in North Dakota." As president, Roosevelt established the U.S. Forest Service, signed the Antiquities Act, created 18 national monuments, and approved five national parks and 51 wildlife refuges.

Roosevelt's ranch and surrounding badlands of the Little Missouri River are now preserved at Theodore Roosevelt National Park in southwestern North Dakota. Buffalo and elk have been

The topography in Badlands is bizarre, and it is also the home of fossils dating back 30 million years. Animals roaming the area then included saber-toothed cats, horses under two feet tall, and ancestors of the rhinoceros.

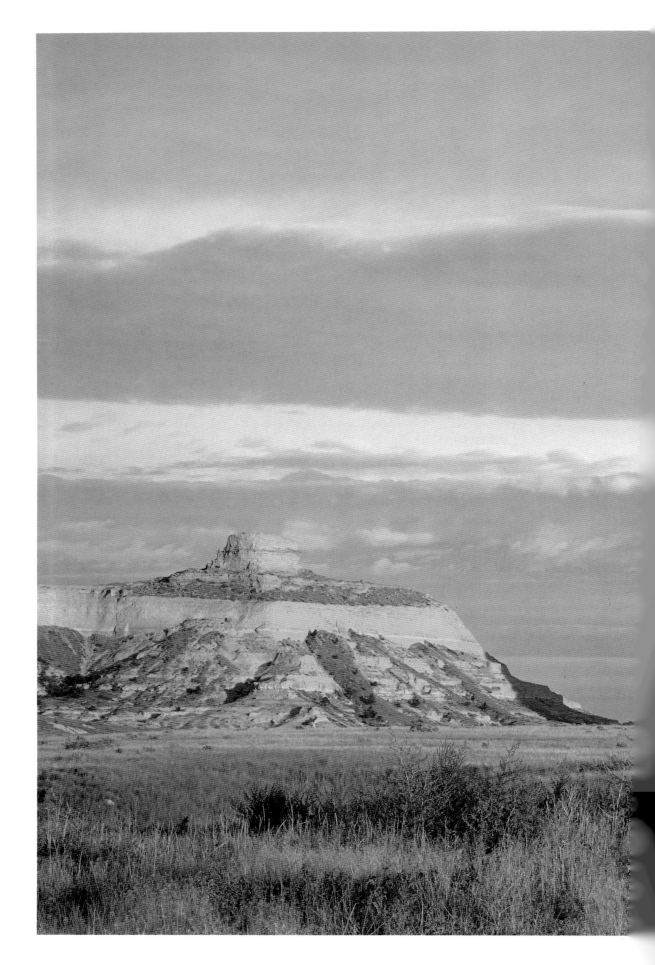

Mitchell Pass, which lies between these rock sentinels in Scotts Bluff National Monument, marks the route of the Oregon Trail that early pioneers took when traveling west across the Nebraska prairie.

Over a period of millions of years, drops of water trickling through fissures in the rock carved out Wind Cave in western South Dakota. Its 37 miles of passageways are concealed under a prairie landscape of hills, ravines, rolling grasslands, and pine forests.

After World War I, as the age of automobile travel boomed, tourists flocked to the national parks. These visitors and Park Service employees pose in front of the cone of Lone Star Geyser in Yellowstone National Park in 1923.

Old Faithful geyser in Yellowstone, the symbol of the world's first national park, puts on its steamy show. It is not the most consistent geyser in the park, nor the most frequent erupter, but it is undoubtedly the most famous and beloved.

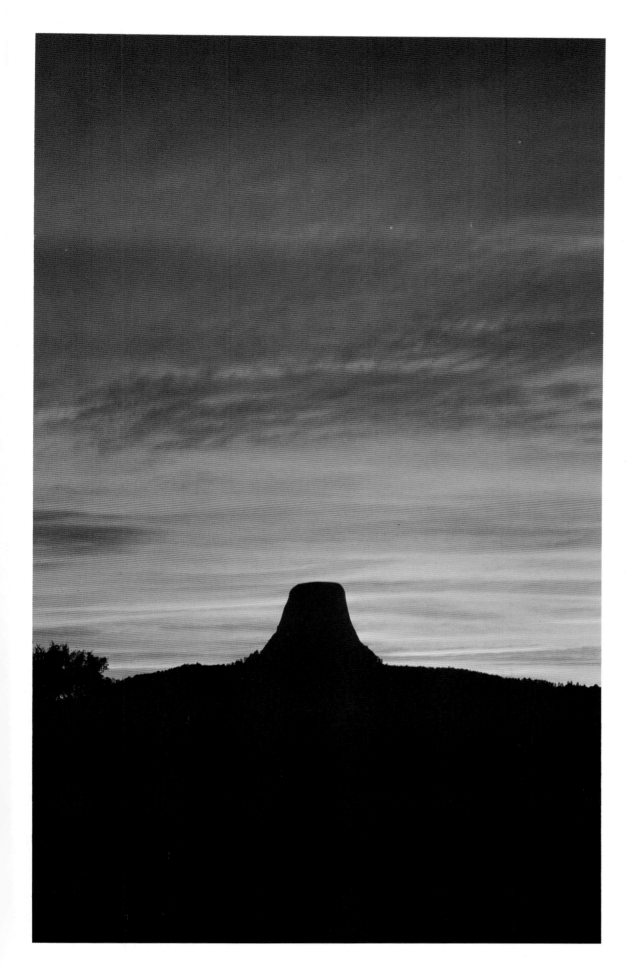

Devils Tower, the nation's first national monument, resembles the stump of a great tree. It is in fact a mass of molten magma that cooled underground, hardened, and formed into hexagonal pillars. Erosion then exposed the tower, which now rises 867 feet from its base.

reintroduced, and the sight of wild horses and Texas longhorns recall the ranching days of a century ago. Prairie dogs peer from their holes, watching for trouble and barking alarms. The meadowlark, "one of our sweetest, loudest songsters," according to Roosevelt, still perches atop a bush where "the Plains air seems to give it a voice." Here, needle and thread grass still bends to the unchallenged wind, and in summer titanic cumulonimbuses still pile up out of nowhere and deposit drenching but welcome rains. The park is a fitting tribute to our first conservation-minded president.

A similar but much larger fragment of the Great Plains has been set aside in Badlands National Park in southwestern South Dakota. Early French-Canadian trappers called the region "bad lands to travel across," but visitors today, provisioned with water, need have no fear of venturing forth afoot or on wheels. Many geological forces, including outwash from highlands to the west and volcanic ash showers, helped create the bizarre shapes of the modern badlands. Although rain is scarce, the force of a few annual thunderstorms tears at the soft strata and shapes the land into a succession of pastel canyons, ridges, chimneys, pillars, toadstools, and other forms.

Weathering has also unmasked fossil evidence of an Oligocene menagerie, almost enough to make us wish we had lived 30 million years ago. We would have wandered among giant pigs, fierce saber-toothed cats, horses only 20 inches tall, rhinoceros ancestors 12 feet tall, and hideous sheeplike creatures sporting three pairs of horns on their faces.

The park lies within the one-time domain of the Dakota, or Sioux, nation, who ruled it aggressively after obtaining horses in the 1700s. The Sioux, in turn, fell before the advancing European-Americans. In 1890, at Stronghold Table within the present park, the Sioux took part in the Ghost Dance ceremony, which promised that the whites would depart and the buffalo would return. Mounting tensions led to tragedy. On December 29 at Wounded Knee, just south of the park, 153 Sioux and 25 soldiers were killed in the last armed conflict involving Native Americans and the U.S.

The Buffalo National River, in Arkansas, is one of the few unpolluted and free-flowing rivers left in the 48 contiguous states. The river is popular with canoeists, who take delight in both its long quiet pools and its whitewater rapids.

Along its length of 132 miles, the Buffalo National River passes numerous springs and bluffs that rise 500 feet. Beyond the river, the area's many caves, sinkholes, waterfalls, and unusual rock formations are typical of the Arkansas Ozarks.

Massive fires swept through Yellowstone National Park in the dry summer of 1988. Hundreds of firefighters worked to extinguish them. These lodgepole pines were charred, and other scars from the flames were likely to remain visible for years, but nature also showed early signs of rebounding from the fires.

Army. The Sioux now participate in the administration of the park.

Today pronghorns, bison, and bighorn sheep roam the land, in far reduced (from the last century) but still welcome numbers. Golden eagles, turkey vultures, and marsh hawks circle the topless sky, watching for prairie dogs and other rodents. Badgers, coyotes, and prairie rattlesnakes join the modern menagerie.

West of the Badlands, in the Black Hills and at the eastern edge of that range are, respectively, Jewel Cave National Monument and Wind Cave National Park. These limestone caverns are among the loveliest anywhere, and with 73 miles of passageway, Jewel Cave is the world's fourth longest. The same upheaval that formed the Black Hills about 60 million years ago cracked the limestone and allowed flowing water to create these awesome subterranean natural art museums.

Jewel Cave is named for its most dramatic feature, the calcite crystals that may sparkle like gems when illuminated. Stalactites and stalagmites have formed and often, as a result of the endless drip, drip, drip of mineral-laden water, one has joined the other to form columns. Water trickling down slanted ceilings has formed translucent draperies, and water spilling over a wall has left deposits of flowstone.

Nearby, one day in 1881, a hunter paused by a hole in the ground and was astonished when a strong wind from the hole blew off his hat. Thus Wind Cave was discovered and got its name. Shifts in atmospheric pressure inside and outside the cave cause the wind to blow first one way, then another. Wind Cave is renowned for its boxwork—the honeycomb-shaped calcite structures that protrude from walls and ceilings—the world's best example of this formation. Other formations include "popcorn," a knobby growth resembling coral, and frostwork, crystals of calcite and argonite that may resemble snowballs.

Norris Geyser Basin is the hottest thermal area in Yellowstone. Altogether, the park has some 10,000 thermal features—geysers, mudpots, hot springs, and fumaroles. The center of the present park collapsed after volcanic eruptions 600,000 years ago, but the smoking and bubbling underground today is a reminder of those violent times.

The Grand Canyon of the Yellowstone River is carved in rhyolite, a volcanic material that spread across the park 600,000 years ago after the eruption of incandescent pumice, ash, and rock particles from Yellowstone Caldera.

The Rocky Mountains, backbone of the continent, extend some 3,200 miles from western Alaska to Sante Fe, New Mexico, and are the most striking physiological feature of the United States and Canada. At the crest of the sequence of ranges, along the invisible line of the Continental Divide, raindrops falling inches apart flow, respectively, toward the Atlantic and Pacific oceans.

Young men who followed Horace Greeley's advice to go west found young mountains composed of very old rock thrown upward and fractured by powerful forces within the earth just 60 million years ago. And the new arrivals who took up prospecting found many treasures buried in the Rockies, including gold, silver, copper, salt, coal, lead, iron, gypsum, gas, and oil shale.

The mountains offered superior visual resources as well, including sharp peaks and rakishly tilted sedimentary formations. Scenes of moisture-filled clouds piling up atop the snow-covered Rockies would have been enough to inspire invention of the picture postcard. The variety and beauty of mountain flora is a dream come true for botanists and photographers. Wild animal herds flourished throughout the high country until most were reduced or wiped out by human predation. It is not surprising that the national park idea was born in the Rockies, in Yellowstone, and it has been advanced through the preservation of other choice mountain landscapes.

Yellowstone has never lost its preeminent position in the hearts and minds of Americans. This is true even though other units in the National Park System are larger and still others are more frequently visited. Yosemite Valley, in its design and detail, has, arguably, a special unsurpassed kind of beauty called grace. A number of parks are wilder than Yellowstone, or more equable in climate.

Yellowstone has many superlatives—10,000 thermal features, for example—but the park cannot be appreciated through these numbers any more than one could understand the importance of Babe Ruth by reciting his stats. Born of legend, its very reality defended only by trappers and prospectors, the least credible of witnesses (as judged by eastern sophisticates), Yellowstone defied probability and emerged from its myths and the mists of its geysers. It emerged finally in its totality as a grand assemblage, an orchestra of nature, plateau and canyon gorge, lakes, and high country, tempestuous in its steamy eruptions yet possessing an ultimate serenity concomitant with its great scale and mountain backdrop. The largest herds south of Alaska—20,000 elk, 2,000 buffalo, plus hundreds of bears, deer, sheep, moose, and pronghorn—are the performers on this great stage.

Flowing out of Yellowstone Lake, the Yellowstone River crosses the park and tumbles down several waterfalls. The Lower Falls, shown here, is 308 feet, twice the height of Niagara Falls. The canyon is up to 1,500 feet deep.

51

Bison (buffalo) graze in a light snowfall at Yellowstone. The park contains the largest animal herds in the United States outside Alaska. Mule deer, moose, elk, black bears, grizzly bears, and bighorn sheep are large mammals that may be seen.

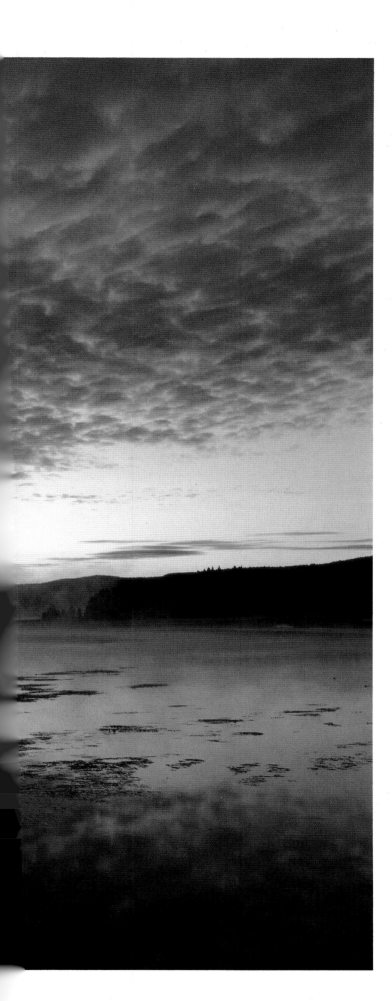

Hayden Valley, in Yellowstone, was named for Ferdinand Hayden, who headed the U.S. Geological and Geographical Survey of the park in 1871 that documented the beauty and uniqueness of the Yellowstone region.

A geyser in Yellowstone. The complex "plumbing" underneath the geysers is not fully understood, and this adds to the mystery of their eruptions.

Americans, millions of whom may never participate in a Loop Road autojam, feel possessive toward Yellowstone, and were incredulous in 1988 when fires burned out of control for months and reportedly "destroyed" much of the park. How could it have been allowed to happen there? The fires, which are an essential part of renewal in nature, did threaten property and park resources and constituted too much of a good thing, but the land rebounded, as opportunistic plants rose from the ashes to be nibbled upon by appreciative wildlife. Americans might redirect their concern to threats involving the grizzly population and the prospective tapping of geothermal energy outside the park that could shut off the eruptions inside the park. Yellowstone's 2.2 million acres are not enough to suit roaming animals, and if the park's resources are to survive, protection must be extended to adjacent national forests now subjected to mining and logging. The park is not yet secure and its future is uncertain.

About those "thermal features." The good news is that geyser function is not fully understood, so we can indulge our imagination a bit. Suffice it to say that the earth's crust is unusually thin under the park, and indeed molten rock churns just two miles beneath the surface. Magma heats the earth, and water flowing through underground cracks then becomes heated, hence lighter, and rises in the vertical tubes of the geysers. The water flashes into steam, which expands into the open-air displays that are unrivaled elsewhere in the world. Each geyser is unique, perhaps erupting hourly, perhaps yearly, some predictably, some without any apparent master plan.

Grand Teton National Park, a short drive to the south over John D. Rockefeller, Jr. Memorial Highway, is associated with Yellowstone in most people's minds, and in fact both are part of the Greater Yellowstone Ecosystem, the largest essentially intact natural area in the earth's temperate zones. Some large mammals migrate seasonally between the parks.

The rocks of the Grand Tetons are ancient, but the mountains themselves are as dynamic and youthful (geologically speaking) as they appear to be. Just nine million years ago, last year's calendar to earth scientists, the ancient rock split into two fault blocks. The faces of the two blocks began to slide against each other, the one to the west rising, the one to the east slipping. For this reason, the eastern face of the Tetons today is stark and abrupt, visible to its base, unobstructed by foothills. A sandstone strip atop Mount Moran, 6,000 feet above the valley floor, once matched up with a layer of sediment now 25,000 feet below the surface of Jackson Hole to the east. Not that you'd notice it, but the Teton Range is still rising, at the rate of a foot every three or four centuries.

Minerva Terrace in the Mammoth Hot Springs area of Yellowstone. Scalding hot water lies only a few inches below the surface of the ground here, and presents a danger to the careless explorer.

The Hot Springs at Yellowstone release great piles of travertine, a form of limestone that often forms terraces. Some of the material welling up from within the earth has created deposits up to 200 feet high.

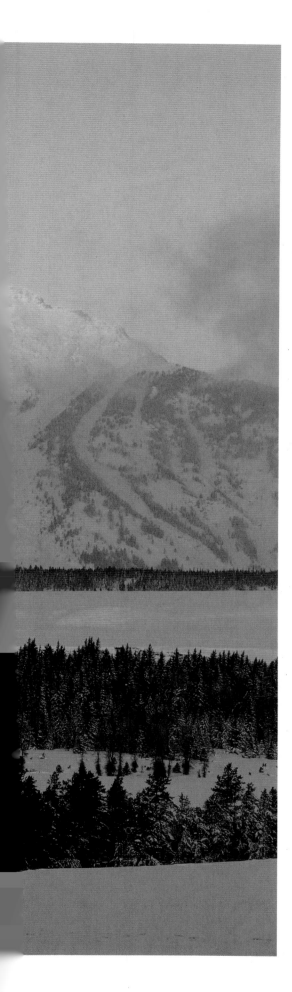

Glaciers pushed through in the much more recent past, but the mountaintops remained unscathed. The broad U-shaped valleys within the mountains and the glacial moraines at their feet evoke the power of the ice sheets.

Topographical features of Jackson Hole include Jackson Lake and many smaller lakes, the meandering Snake River, and buttes that rise from the valley. Wildflowers, often in carpets, spread across the valley in season, and conifers cling to the steep sides of the mountains.

Bald eagles and ospreys fish and nest along the river. Spring brings great blue herons to their rookery at Oxbow Bend. Migratory waterfowl rely on the ponds formed by the constructions of beavers. Nearly 3,000 elk spend the summer in the park, then move south to the National Elk Refuge after snow begins to fall. Bison meander through the sagebrush country south of Jackson Lake, and moose work the rivers and streams, consuming aquatic plants. Mule deer and coyotes are prominent, but the bighorn sheep stay out of sight high on the mountains.

Rocky Mountain National Park, which encompasses a portion of the Front (eastern) Range of the Rockies in Colorado, provides a unique opportunity: easy access for most visitors to the lonely world of alpine tundra. The means of access for most visitors is Trail Ridge Road, a 50-mile-long scenic route that tops out at 12,183 feet, well above the tree line. The highest point in the park is the crest of Longs Peak, with an altitude of 14,255 feet.

The word "fragile," sometimes overused in describing various kinds of landscapes, seems altogether apt for the wind-whipped tundra of stunted plants and bare rock. The wind is so strong that the dried-out terrain is in effect a desert. The temporary absence of a snow cover allows a growing season that can be less than ten weeks long. Lichens and mosses cling to the exposed rock.

A winter sunrise adds a delicate beauty to the jagged peaks of the Grand Tetons, which provide perhaps the most stunning view of the Rocky Mountains along their entire eastern façade.

The dunes in Great Sand Dunes National Monument, containing some of the largest and highest in the United States, were formed in southern Colorado by winds blowing through passes in the lofty Sangre de Cristo Mountains.

A beaver dam has created a pool in Jackson Hole, the broad valley in Grand Teton National Park that attracts a wildlife menagerie.

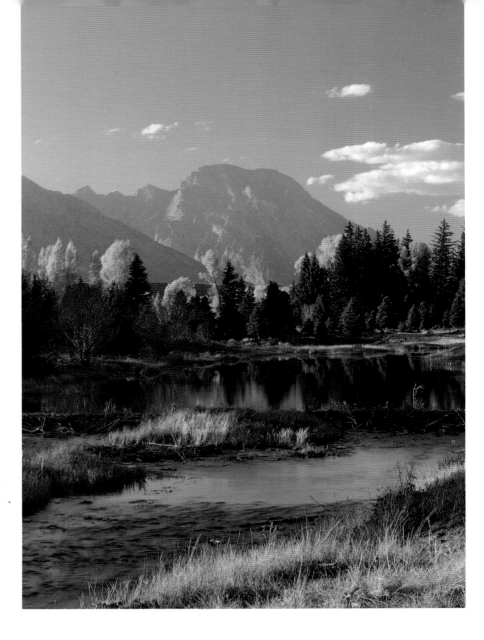

A view of Grand Teton from the Cascade Canyon trail, which leads from Jenny Lake in Jackson Hole up into the mountains to Lake Solitude, and then over 10,720-foot Paintbrush Divide.

Rocky Mountain National Park in Colorado embraces the highest mountain in the southern Rockies. Bear Lake is a popular destination in a park that also includes the Trail Ridge Road, the nation's highest paved highway.

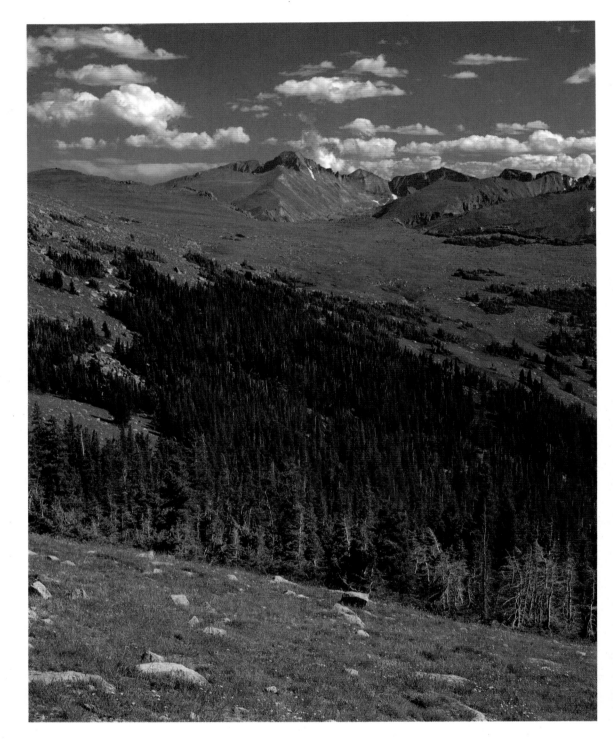

The high-elevation backcountry in Rocky Mountain National Park is an open door for hikers, and in fact there are 355 miles of trails. One-third of the park is above the tree line, and here the tundra, more common in far-northern latitudes, dominates the landscape.

Mammalian life is surprisingly vigorous. Two herds of bighorns, symbols of the park, but now reduced to only 200 individuals, roam the high country. Pocket gophers perform the good deed of churning the soil. Pikas store dried grasses in sheltered dens. Weasels and marmots scurry about. Among birds, only the ptarmigan spends the entire year above the tree line.

Waterton/Glacier International Peace Park sprawls across the international boundary between Alberta and Montana. Glacier National Park, on the American side, and its Canadian counterpart share similar high-mountain scenery, long and thin glacier-carved lakes, and abundant flora and fauna.

The region contains primarily sedimentary rock—mudstone, sandstone, and limestone. Long after deposition, Precambrian rock to the west, a billion years old, was pushed up, and it slid 40 miles to the northeast until it rode over younger rock, creating an overthrust, an awesome rearranging of geological furniture. Today the overthrust rock has become the Lewis Range, easternmost in the park, and it rises dramatically above the adjacent prairie.

Erosion worked on this design, and ice invaded the future park four times, scooping out valleys and pushing debris before it that now stands as hilly glacial moraines. Some 50 glaciers remain from the ice sheets, occupying amphitheaters, or cirques, high on the mountainsides.

Two hundred lakes and hundreds of waterfalls are additional gifts of the ice age. Virgin forests scale the mountains, and in autumn, the yellow mass of quaking aspen lights up the landscape. During the fall some 350 migrating golden and bald eagles fly down to McDonald Creek to feast on Kokanee salmon. Glacier is another of the few remaining redoubts of the grizzly and bighorn. Mountain goats, sporting long shaggy white coats and upturned black horns, are at home on the steep slopes. The Going-to-the-Sun Road is the scenic rival to Rocky Mountain's Trail Ridge Road, though it ascends only to 6,664 feet at Logan Pass.

Mount Grinnell rises sharply from Grinnell Lake in Glacier National Park. Some 50 glaciers, souvenirs of the most recent visit by sheets of ice, still occupy amphitheaters and cirques, high in the mountains.

Canyons and Deserts

Turret Arch stands beyond the North Window in Arches National Park. Moisture, wind, gravity, and the roots of small plants help work open the holes in the fins of rock, a very slow geological process.

A gnarled juniper, a familiar tree of the Colorado Plateau, clings to the edge of a cliff in Colorado National Monument. Beyond Grand Valley, the Book Cliffs shine in the last light before sunset.

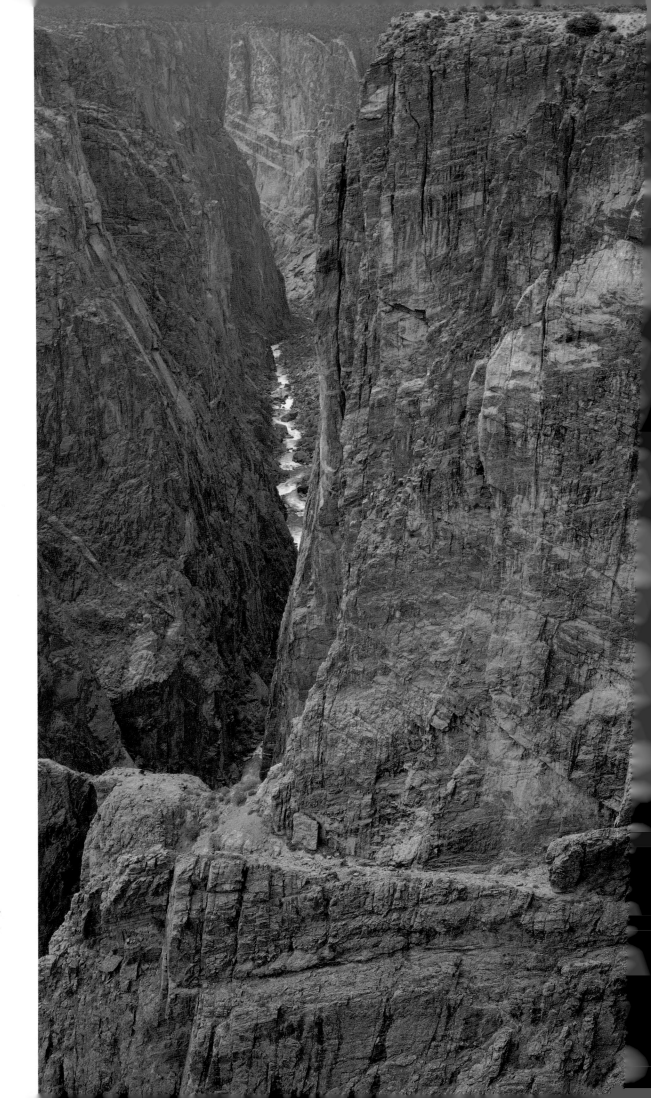

Black Canyon of the Gunnison National Monument includes a portion of this gorge in Western Colorado. The Gunnison is part of the Colorado River drainage, famous for its awesome canyons. Sunlight often fails to penetrate this chasm, hence the name Black Canyon.

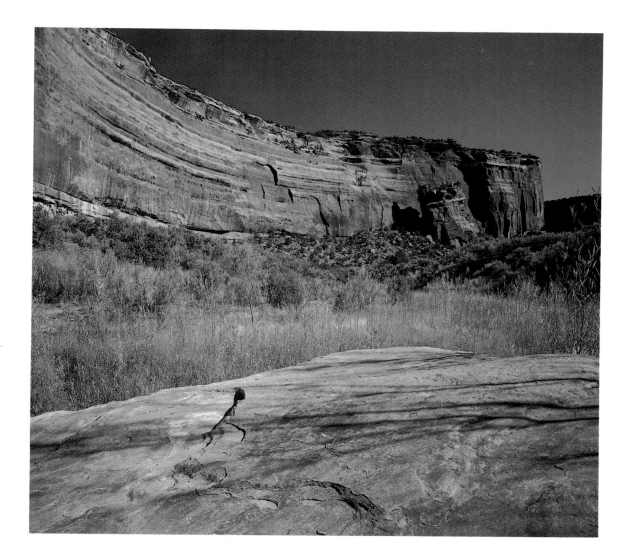

The Colorado and Gunnison rivers unite at Grand Junction, Colorado, and here also the Colorado breaks out of the Rocky Mountains and begins its stupendous job of carving the deep canyons of the Colorado Plateau. One of its first artistic "assignments" is at Colorado National Monument, which contains this graceful concave wall.

Millions of years ago, in eastern Utah, the bodies of dinosaurs were washed down a river, and they piled up on a river bank. The remains have fossilized into an almost scary jumble of leg bones and backbones.

A desert, by strict definition, is an area receiving no more than ten inches of precipitation per year. Not all of the American Southwest thus qualifies as desert, and indeed green oases freshen the landscape. But the overall perception is one of dryness, of burning sun and naked rock and empty arroyos, of wind that sings as it churns up stinging grains of sand, of cracked earth and lined faces, of lizards scurrying for shade and furtive mammals—hunters and hunted—who venture forth only in the cool of the night.

To those who linger in the desert long enough to fall in love with it, a far more complex and subtle picture emerges. Plants and animals in surprising variety have all developed strategies for surviving in the harsh climate. The rocks themselves tell a story of hundreds of millions of years of geological change that can be read with pleasure by observant explorers.

And finally it is water itself, in scarce supply but by no means absent, that ultimately shapes and designs the arid lands and provides its most dramatic moments. The joke about the so-called two-inch rain—the raindrops fall two inches apart—reflects the frustration of cattlemen and dirt farmers who need an occasional break from the sunlight. But rain really does come, often all at once. One can stand at the edge of the Grand Canyon or at some other vantage point and see three or more thunderstorms in progress.

Rain can be gentle, but it is more often drenching, and as the rainwater spills across the hard earth and pours into dry streambeds, flash floods occur. The roiling mass of opaque water, snagging outcrops of dirt and small trees and other debris as it surges forward, eventually enters larger creeks and pushes onto one of the desert's major rivers. The Colorado and the Rio Grande are the master streams. These drainages, including their myriad tributaries, have sculptured the land, producing the distinct shapes of buttes, mesas, and canyons. The Colorado system, in particular, has created an infinitude of curious rock forms.

To trace the Colorado from its source is to take a trip through two billion years of geological time. Such a journey also takes the traveler along a nearly unbroken chain of starkly beautiful parklands. "The River of the Shining Mountains" rises in the Never Summer Range near the Continental Divide in central Colorado, and works its way southwest, picking up side stream flows in a fairly conventional manner until it breaks out of the Rockies and rips into the sedimentary strata of the Colorado Plateau. Colorado National Monument, near the Utah border, is just a 20,000-acre sandstone tease, its walls and monoliths a bare hint of what is to come.

The serious scenery begins inside Utah as the river deepens its channel and forms most of the southern border of Arches National Park. The Great Sculptor took his (or her) time in forming the

Double Arch in Arches National Park. More than 200 of these rock openings have been found in this park, the largest collection of arches in the world.

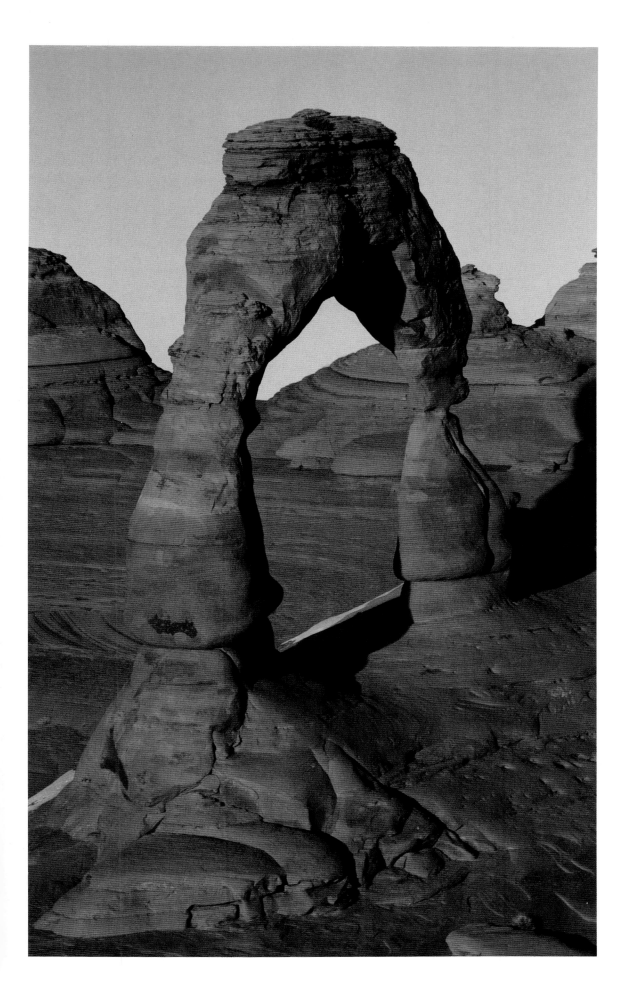

Delicate Arch, well concealed in the slickrock wilderness of eastern Utah, is the symbol of Arches National Park. Stained by traces of iron, the bare sandstone glows brightly at sunrise and sunset.

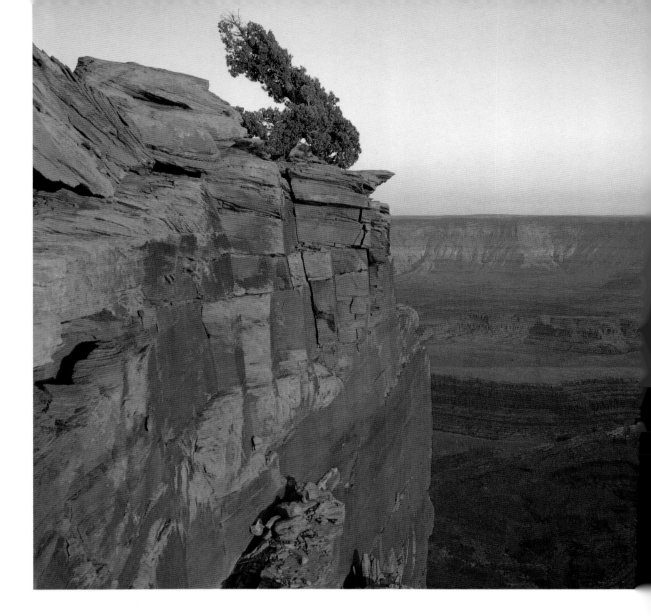

Below Dead Horse Point, the Colorado River meanders toward its confluence with the Green River deep within the rock wilderness of Canyonlands National Park. To appreciate the power of the river in eroding rock, consider that the stone buttress at left was once connected in an unbroken layer with its "sister" mesa beyond the river.

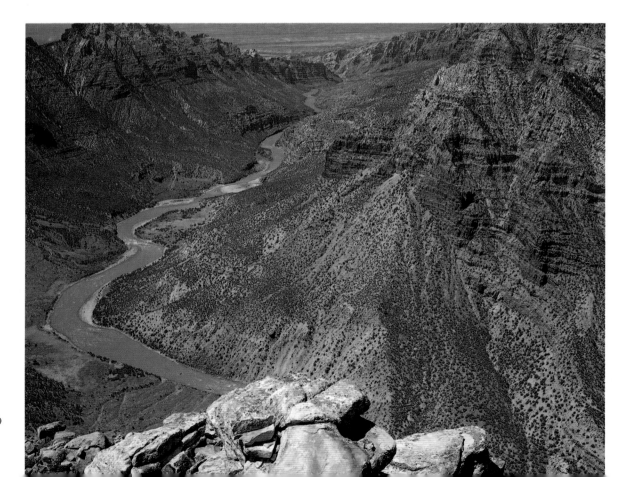

The Green River, another tributary of the Colorado, has carved deeply into the ancient rock formations in Dinosaur National Monument and revealed the fossils of more giant reptiles.

200 or so openings in the rock that the park contains today—the world's largest collection of stone arches. The story begins 300 million years ago when an ocean basin formed and salt deposits accumulated at the bottom of the basin. Massive deposits of sand and sediments spread atop the 3,000 feet of salt and hardened into stone. The weight pushed the salt down in places, but the salt was forced up elsewhere if the rock cover was thinner. The upward pressure and subsequent regional uplift cracked the rock in a sequence of long parallel lines called joints. The rock might be likened to sliced bread, but with the slices still together as in a loaf. Gradually water and ice and the roots of plants worked into the joints and began to leverage the slices apart. They became freestanding fins. Then more weathering typically occurred at the base of the fins and pieces of the rock fell away to produce holes. Gravity and further weathering opened the holes to create arches.

Landscape Arch, at 291 feet, is so thin that it might snap in two at any time—maybe even in the next million years.

The prize among arches requires some effort, a fairly steep ascent up a slickrock slope through a multicolored rock jungle, then a careful walk along a narrow ledge on a sheer cliff, and then…it appears, Delicate Arch, a staple of landscape calendars, perfect in its shape and scale, poised on

Rain is infrequent in Canyonlands National Park, but it often falls in a downpour. Some of the runoff will remain in waterpockets in the rock for awhile. Small crustaceans such as fairy shrimp will hatch from eggs in a waterpocket; they mature, mate, and lay eggs before the water evaporates, ending their brief lives.

The Green River, in the distance, flows through the park. Rafters and kayakers spend days on this placid stretch of the river, admiring the multicolored cliffs and ancient Anasazi ruins and rock paintings.

Below Grand View Point in Canyonlands National Park lies the White Rim, and the rim itself is fracturing into the many pinnacles of Monument Basin.

the lip of a deep sandstone bowl, framing the distant—sometimes snow-covered—LaSal Mountains, and glowing orange in the late afternoon sun. Hikers sit mesmerized, stunned, out of breath in its presence. No photograph can do it justice because Delicate Arch can be appreciated fully only along with the totality of its setting—the stone wilderness rolling away in every direction, primeval, uncompromising, endless for all one can tell, uncivilized majesty.

Arches National Park lies northeast of the town of Moab, the obvious base for exploring the wild country of eastern Utah. (The scenery, it should be noted, doesn't stop at the boundaries of the parks.) The Colorado River swings past Moab and, after more goosenecking, enters Canyonlands National Park. This park is a canyon country Louvre, a museum preserving much of what makes the Southwest special. Here one can find some of the world's most important examples of primitive rock paintings, some of the most dramatic deep canyon scenery, and surely the world's most extravagant collection of geological sculpture.

The Green and Colorado rivers unite within the park, and the Confluence Overlook becomes a mecca for surefooted hikers who look down into the shadows and try to understand how the two rivers could have wrought such erosional destruction. South of the confluence, the Colorado enters Cataract Canyon, where it drops eight feet per mile, a steeper rate than in the Grand Canyon.

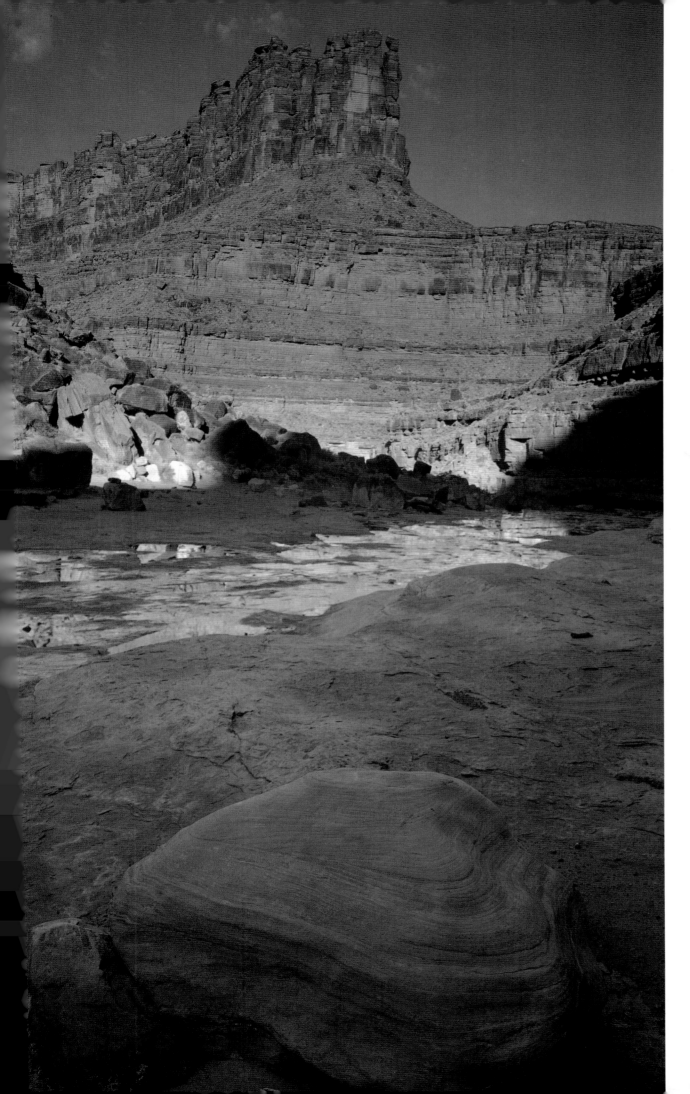

Within Glen Canyon National Recreation Area in Utah, Lake Powell and the San Juan River provide access by boat to intriguing side canyons, including Slickborn Canyon. The striations of the rocks reveal the many layers of sediments laid down by ancient rivers, lakes, and seas.

75

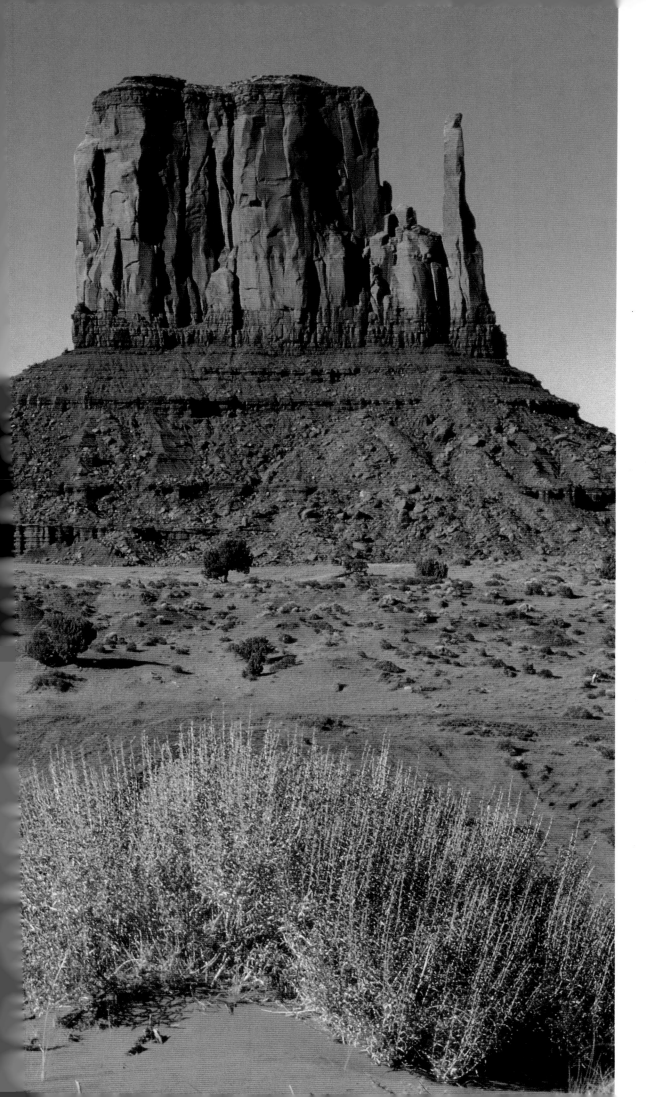

One of the "Mittens" and other striking stone formations rise boldly from the lay of the land in Monument Valley Navajo Tribal Park. Administered by the Navajo, this park, which lies across the Arizona-Utah border, is not a part of the National Park System.

Almost 200 miles long, Lake Powell fills the channel of the Colorado River and many of its tributaries. The lake meets the ambitious goals set for it, storing water and generating power. It is also heavily used for waterborne recreation.

Owachomo is one of three massive stone bridges in Natural Bridges National Monument in southeastern Utah. A bridge, unlike a natural arch, is formed when flowing water works its way through a tall slender fin of rock. Erosion then expands the opening to form a graceful natural bridge.

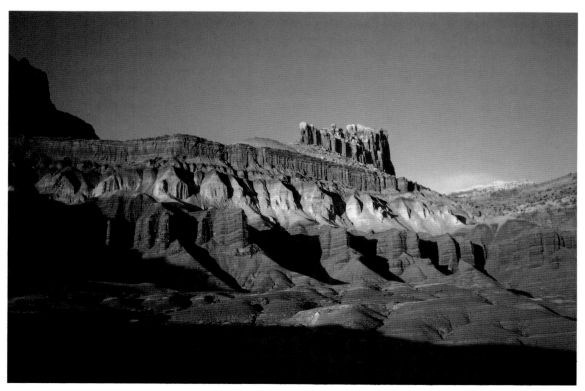

The Castle, along the Waterpocket Fold, in Capitol Reef National Park, Utah. Along the western façade of the fold, which extends for about 100 miles, hundreds of millions of years of geological history are revealed in a sequence of rock strata.

Thrill-seekers in rubber rafts floating through the Big Drop descend thirty feet in one mile, a degree of slope offering an experience that may seem comparable to falling down a flight of stairs. Most rafters pay outfitters for the privilege.

Canyonlands has few miles of paved roads, and the dirt roads are so malevolent you might rather walk. The park is a wilderness without the saving grace of handsome green forests. It is a paradox—so formidable to approach that it becomes a challenge to be met, so grotesque in design that it becomes compellingly beautiful.

River rafters, hardly recovered from the trauma of the Big Drop, soon encounter an almost unsettling calm. The forward movement of the raft ceases and the froth of the whitewater fades. The voyagers have exited the park and entered Glen Canyon National Recreation Area, which is synonymous with Lake Powell. The motor is turned on and the raft proceeds to the takeout landing. Lake Powell is almost 200 miles long.

A trip southwest on the lake brings one past tributaries of the buried river that lead to other natural shrines. Natural Bridges National Monument, to the south, contains three huge stone bridges. These may resemble arches but they are created by the flow of water in a streambed. During flash floods, rushing water moving through a loop in a stream course slams into a tall fin of rock and eventually punches a hole in the rock. The water then takes a short cut, rushing through the hole and enlarging it. Weathering further widens the opening, and a natural bridge is the result.

The Dirty Devil River enters Lake Powell from the north, and one of its tributaries, the Fremont River, courses through the Waterpocket Fold, the principal geological feature of Capitol Reef National Park.

For centuries Native Americans have lived in the deep gorges of Canyon de Chelly National Monument. Navajo farmers still live in their simple homes on the canyon floor, and hikers may not enter most of the canyon without a Navajo guide.

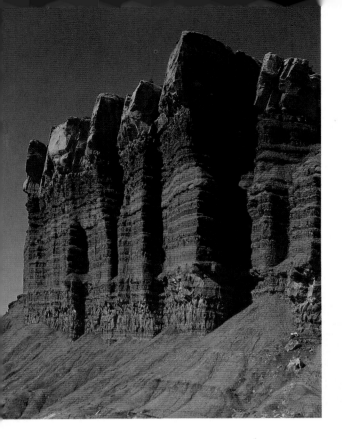

The Egyptian Temple, in Utah's Capitol Reef National Park, is carved mostly in the Moenkopi Formation, which consists of sandstone, siltstones, and mudstones laid down some 200 million years ago. Fossils of ancient marine animals can be found in the rock.

Long after white Americans began settling in the desert, Rainbow Bridge remained just a rumor, a mysterious place sacred to Native Americans living in the vicinity of the Arizona-Utah border. Finally, led by two Paiute guides, whites traveled by horseback in 1909 overland through brutal, hazardous terrain and finally saw this magnificent bridge.

The Fold, about 100 miles long and nearly straight as an arrow for most of its length, was created 60 million years ago when earth forces pushed up sedimentary rock and left it pointed upward to the west at about a forty-five degree angle. Time then eroded a portion of the rock, and what is left thrusts boldly out of the ground as one of the most spectacular landforms in the United States. The western façade of the fold is a geological textbook, written in stone.

At the base of the fold are the chocolate-colored sandstones, siltstones, and mudstones of the Moenkopi Formation. Ripple marks left in the sand by the lapping waters at a shoreline are still dramatically visible 200 million years later. Amphibians swimming in the shallow water slapped the sand with their fins and these fin marks are visible today.

The Moenkopi is topped in places by the Shinarump Conglomerate. Its sometimes hummocky appearance gave rise to its irreverent name: Shinar is the Paiute word for wolf, and rump is an English slang word needing no elaboration. The Shinarump, representing the deposits of stream-beds, is a source of uranium that is found in its petrified wood. The Shinarump is the bottom layer of the Chinle Formation, which comes from various watery environments and volcanic ash. The Chinle forms gentle soft mounds in pastels of green, gray, pink, blue, and purple.

The massive sheer cliffs of Wingate sandstone rise hundreds of feet above the Chinle and flame

The Kolob Canyon section of Zion National Park is a remote primitive area where backpackers survive on water they carry or rely on a few springs where water spills out of the rock.

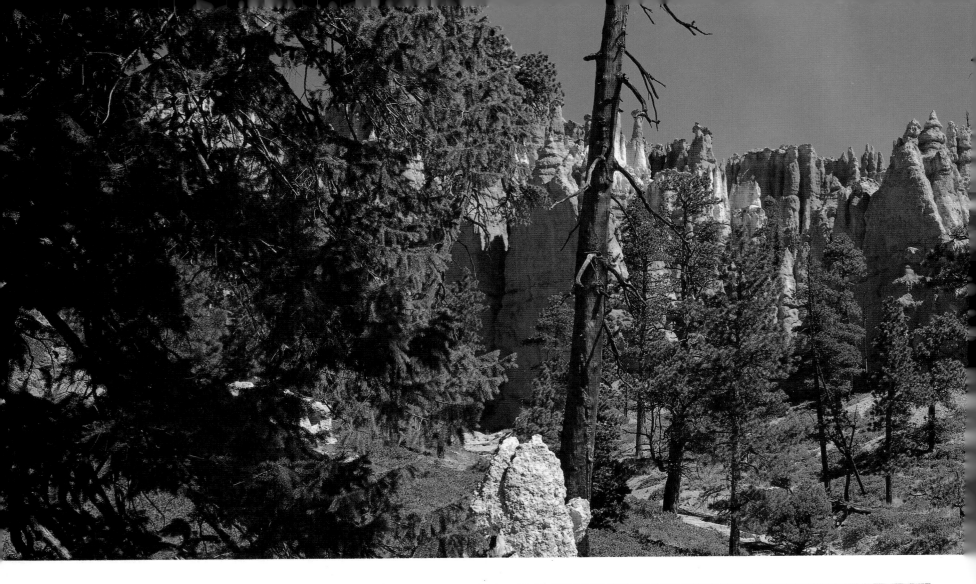

The bizarre formations of Bryce Canyon recall the comment of the man, on seeing a giraffe for the first time, that "there ain't no such animal." Perhaps no area on the face of the earth surpasses the canyonlands of Utah and Arizona in the color and design of its sculptured rock formations.

The pinnacles of Bryce Canyon National Park in southern Utah represent nature in one of its most creative moments. The display runs on for 20 miles in a large horseshoe-shaped amphitheater (not a canyon) above the Paunsaugunt Plateau.

brightly in the late sunlight. As the soft underlying Chinle erodes away, the Wingate breaks off in giant blocks that scatter across the terrain. The Kayenta Formation, atop the Wingate, resembles it in color and shape. The Wingate-Kayenta cliffs are usually stained by long dark stripes of desert varnish, which may be formed when water carrying concentrations of manganese and iron spills down the face of the cliff. The ancients scratched petroglyphs into the varnished surfaces, using the lighter rock beneath to achieve a pleasing artistic effect.

The Navajo Sandstone domes top off the Waterpocket Fold. The Navajo was delivered to the canyon country 175 million years ago by winds that blew first one way and then another. These shifts in direction are still evident in the many-angled cross-bedding in this sandstone. The Navajo domes resemble the domes of capitol buildings, giving Capitol Reef part of its name. "Reef" is a reference to the Fold itself.

Rainbow Bridge, the world's largest and undoubtedly most beautiful natural bridge, spans a side canyon off Lake Powell, and is easily accessible by boat. *Nonnezoshi,* Navajo for "rainbow of stone," arches upward 290 feet, and the U.S. Capitol building could be placed beneath it.

Below Glen Canyon Dam, just across the border in Arizona, the Paria River enters from the north. The Paria heads at the base of the amphitheater beneath the thousands of slender, graceful formations in a panoply of colors that constitute Bryce Canyon National Park.

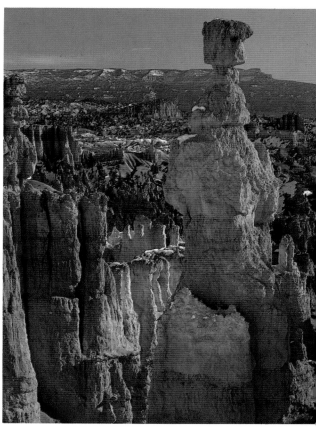

Thor's Hammer, from Sunset Point, in Bryce Canyon. The soft strata were deposited by a lake that covered the area. The delicate color of the spires complements perfectly their fragile shape.

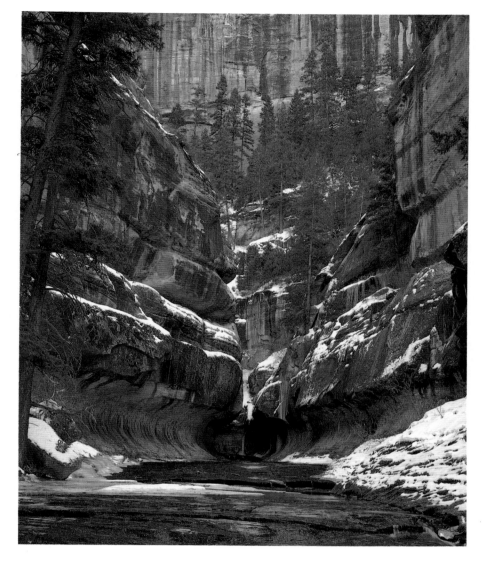

Zion is renowned for several deep slots in the earth that provide challenging backpack trips which often require explorers to wade in water. This is Great West Canyon.

Elves Chasm, a side canyon off the Colorado River in the Grand Canyon, may be well named: the elves who live here have undoubtedly developed a special love for this enchanting place.

Bryce Canyon is better seen than written about, because language has no words to describe adequately its spectacle, the sheer mass of its pinnacles and spires and the delicacy of its colors. The formations one sees today were laid down as silt at the bottom of a lake. The soft siltstone has eroded readily under pressure of falling rain and of ice expanding between cracks in the rock. Iron (adding reds) and manganese (adding blues and lavenders) have colored the rock.

The Paiute name for Bryce translates as "Red rocks standing like men in a bowl-shaped canyon." That's rather straightforward, and no wordsmith can improve upon it.

Zion, the westernmost of Utah's five national parks, has been shaped largely by the Virgin River, another tributary of the Colorado. The speed with which running water sculptures the land depends on what kind of rock it must contend with. The dominant rock layer at Zion is the Navajo Sandstone, which at Capitol Reef forms the domes above the Waterpocket Fold. In Zion, the Navajo is nearly one-half mile in thickness. The Great White Throne and other formations in Zion Canyon are carved in this sandstone. Throughout the canyon, water working its way through the porous sandstone spills and trickles down the cliffs, and hanging gardens of columbine, monkeyflower, and other plants decorate the rock walls.

Further up Zion Canyon, the river is forced to cut through the much more resistant Kayenta Formation. Here the canyon narrows to 20 feet in width, and it is 2,000 feet in depth. These narrows, some 16 miles in length, provide one of the spookiest, most memorable hikes in the Southwest. One must wade through the stream channel, which is often filled with water wall to wall.

The half-mile climb from the canyon floor and the hiking available in Zion's vast backcountry reward the energetic explorer.

The Grand Canyon, nature's most ambitious excavation project, extends for 277 miles through the plateau of northern Arizona. Many millions of people from around the world have stood at the rims and stared at the canyon, and a far smaller number have walked down into the gorge or floated through it. Occasionally a tourist can be heard to exclaim, "There's a river down there!" Many visitors have only the gauziest idea of what they're looking at or how it got that way. They choose simply to savor the beauty of the canyon, as when the mesas and buttes rising within the gorge are touched by the early or late sun or when they are skiffed with snow.

Unlike the Grand Canyon, which one customarily views from the rims, Zion Canyon in Zion National Park is accessible primarily from the valley floor, and visitors can savor the power and beauty of the rock walls rising high above their heads.

Curtains of clouds rise and fall above the Grand Canyon, adding to the drama of the scene on display below. The changing interplay of light and cloud throughout the day and the seasons ensures that the canyon will always be different in appearance.

The canyon in winter suffers from less air pollution, and snow enhances its beauty. With far few visitors on hand, the solitude is overwhelming.

The rocks in the Grand Canyon are very old—up to two billion years old at the bottom of the canyon, some of the oldest rocks exposed anywhere on the earth. And yet, the canyon itself is quite young, geologically speaking, having been scooped out by the Colorado River in about seven million years.

In the 1960s the leaders of the environmental movement narrowly prevented Federal approval of the construction of a dam in the Grand Canyon. Such a dam would have ruined the natural appearance of the canyon. It would also have ended the downcutting of the river through the gorge, one of the most dramatic ongoing stories in geological history.

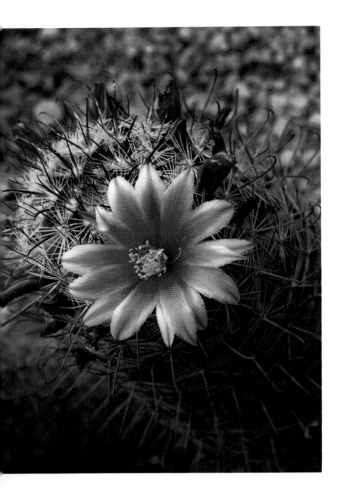

But any understanding of the abyss, let alone a heightened appreciation of its beauty, requires one to consider the canyon as a chronicle of life on earth. At the rim you can observe seashells deposited in the limestone a mere 250 million years ago. But at the bottom, a vertical mile below the South Rim, you can touch granite two billion years old, appropriately black, and devoid of fossils because it was created in a world that knew no life in any form. When walking out of the canyon on foot, remember that each step up the trail represents a thousand years of earth history. Hikers must climb up past the remains of the crablike trilobites, past the age of fishes, and through a limestone graveyard containing the crushed remains of myriad oysterlike creatures. They then walk among the footprints of short-legged amphibians, past delicate fossil tracings of primitive ferns in which a few insect-wings commingle, and up the frozen dunes of the Coconino sandstone.

The climb brings hikers to three life zones otherwise widely distributed across the face of the earth. These are the Lower Sonoran Zone with its agave, cactus, yucca, lizards, and rattlesnakes; the Upper Sonoran Zone, featuring the dwarf forest of pinyon and juniper; and the Transition Zone, with its ponderosa groves enlivened by the calls of the chickadee and the Steller's jay. Perhaps it is this double and concurrent passage, through geological time and biological space, in this extraordinary setting, that enables the explorer to transcend the customary limits of a three-dimensional world.

A different kind of passage through the canyon, by rubber raft or wooden dory, carries the courageous through one or two weeks of whitewater—the world's premier waterborne adventure. In quiet moments, perhaps after beaching at a sandy campsite, one can explore the unknown worlds of hanging waterfalls and bottomless swimming pools in sinuous side canyons too narrow to receive the direct illumination of the sun.

The bright flower of the pincushion cactus, Saguaro National Monument.

A barrel cactus, displaying a hands-off attitude, gets a colorful early start in Saguaro National Monument in southern Arizona.

The Sonoran Desert in Organ Pipe Cactus National Monument in southern Arizona harbors many unusual plants, including the pencil-shaped saguaro cactus and the many-armed organ pipe cactus. The area has little water, and Spanish explorers called a route through the region El Camino del Diablo—The Devil's Highway.

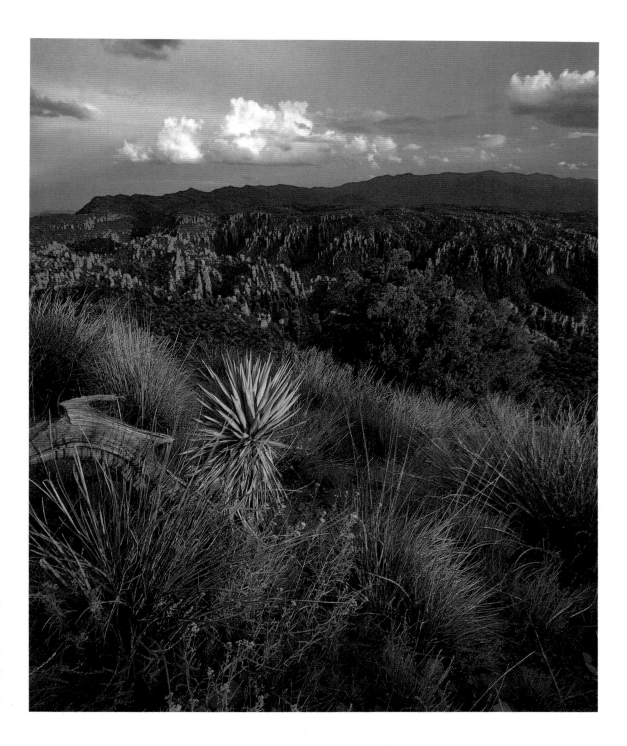

Chiricahua National Monument contains a fantasy world that the Chiricahua Apaches called the Land of the Standing-Up Rocks. The upright stones are being eroded out of the Chiricahua Mountains. They consist of rhyolite, a rock formed from volcanic ash that spewed out of a nearby caldera.

Full-grown saguaro cacti, like these in the national monument, have several branching arms. Woodpeckers, owls, and other birds excavate holes in the cacti for their nests, which are up to 20°F cooler in summer than the "outside" temperature.

Near the bottom of the Grand Canyon, the Havasupai, the "people of the blue-green water," live in the village of Supai, accessible only by a 65-mile road and an eight-mile trip by horseback or afoot down a precipitous trail.

Exiting from the Grand Canyon, the Colorado River flows west into Lake Mead National Recreation Area. The lake was created by construction of Hoover Dam, one of the world's most remarkable engineering achievements, on the Arizona-Nevada border. Below the dam the diminished river resumes its course south toward the Gulf of California. The states through which it passes withdraw huge quantities of its water for irrigation and power, reducing the river to barely a trickle as it crosses into Mexico. The demise of the Colorado, short of the open sea, is a sad end for the river that, with its tributaries, has given form to a dozen national parks and monuments.

Four national parks lie within the drainage of the Southwest's other master stream, the Rio Grande.

Colorful badlands topography similar to that found in the Dakotas is protected in Petrified Forest National Park in northeastern Arizona. The park includes a portion of the Painted Desert, with its rocks colored red, pink, purple, lavender, pale green, chocolate, and gray. Two hundred million years ago, many streams flowed through the area, which was populated by animals resembling alligators and hippopotamuses, not to mention dinosaurs. Fossils of the enduring, if not endearing, cockroach have also turned up.

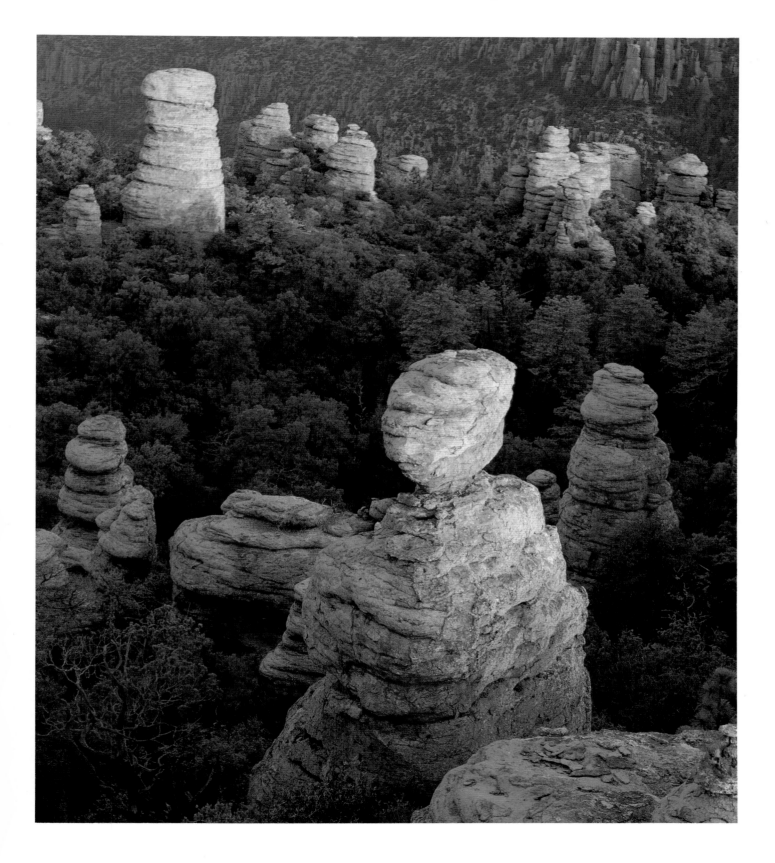

Sunrise illuminates the stone figures in Chiricahua National Monument. From these rugged, isolated mountains, Apaches led by Cochise and Geronimo attacked pioneer travelers and settlers.

The soft badlands strata in the Petrified
Forest erode quickly, and new fossils of
trees and prehistoric animals emerge from
the ground frequently.

In Petrified Forest National Park, in
northern Arizona, erosion has uncovered
the fossilized remains of towering 200
million-year-old trees. Deposits of silica,
which replaced the wood, provide the
brilliant colors seen today.

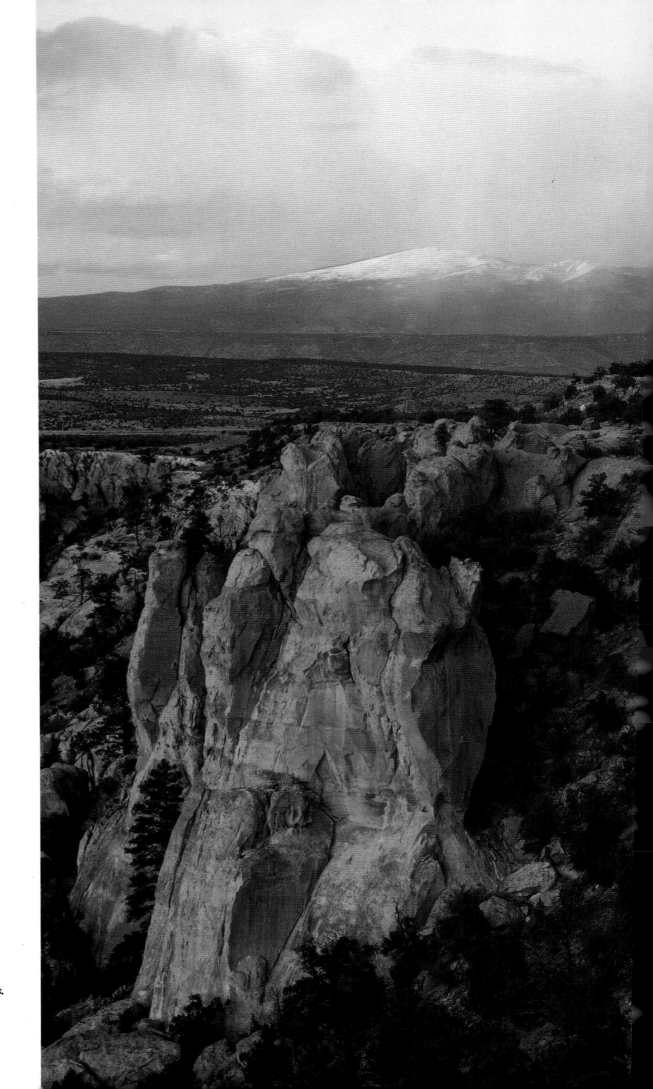

El Malpais National Monument in northwestern New Mexico is a recent (1987) addition to the National Park System. Its many unusual erosional forms have been created out of volcanic deposits.

The park was established to protect rather more fascinating fossils, those of conifers up to 200 feet tall that toppled over and were washed by swollen streams into a floodplain. Silt, mud, and volcanic ash covered the trunks, cutting off oxygen and slowing the decay of the trees. Ground waters bearing silica seeped through the logs and replaced the original wood tissues with silica deposits. The silicas hardened and the logs became petrified wood.

Harder rock covered the area, and it in turn was eroded away. Now the soft strata containing the fossil logs have been exposed. The logs have broken into chunks in a variety of sizes and a riot of color. Here, the erosion is swift, and each gullywasher brings with it the promise of new surprises. In 1984 a large dinosaur nicknamed Gertie turned up, and scientists are still trying to figure out whether this lizard-like animal was indeed a true reptile.

El Malpais National Monument, added to the Park System in 1987, is an eerie northwestern New Mexico landscape that shows the marks of volcanic violence. This seldom-seen wilderness contains cinder mountains, hollow lava tubes as large as subway passages, and caves filled with ice that never melts.

In southern New Mexico, White Sands National Monument showcases the world's largest gypsum dunefield, covering 230 square miles. The brilliant white dunes rise to 60 feet in height.

Farther south the Guadalupe Mountains, which lie across the New Mexico-Texas border, are home to two national parks, one in each state. In New Mexico, the Carlsbad Caverns were formed

Pre-Columbian petroglyphs and Pueblo Indian ruins have been found among the rock formations in El Morro National Monument in northwestern New Mexico. Inscription Rock contains the carved signatures of Spanish explorers and early 19th century immigrants and settlers.

The underground passageways in Carlsbad Caverns National Park contain an unusually large array of formations, including stalagmites, stalactites, soda straws, draperies, flowstone, cave pearls, and popcorn.

within a great reef of rock. Rainwater, acidified by air and soil, worked its way beneath the surface and dissolved underground limestone chambers. The creation of decorations within the cave, including draperies, flowstone, and cave pearls, has taken place in the last 500,000 years, all the result of water dripping into the cave. Each drop leaves a crystal of calcite, the building block of the decorations.

During spring, summer, and early fall, 300,000 Mexican free-tail bats live in the caves, sleeping by day attached to the ceiling. One square foot may contain up to 300 bats. At dusk, they exit the caverns en masse to hunt for insects.

The Guadalupe Mountains are part of an ancient marine fossil reef—one of the world's finest examples. Incongruous as it seems today, as one stands in the desert, the reef was formed underwater, by sponges and other marine organisms that secreted lime. The sea evaporated, and the reef was buried under other sediments until the whole area was uplifted and the reef partly re-exposed. Guadalupe Mountains National Park incorporates the highlands, canyons, and portions of the surrounding desert. In The Bowl, a forested depression atop the mountains, elk, deer, mountain lions, and black bears roam. McKittrick Canyon is a verdant spring-fed oasis that has been called "the most beautiful spot in Texas."

Big Bend National Park is named for the lazy U-shape in the Rio Grande, which forms 107 miles of the park's southern boundary separating Texas and Mexico. The deep limestone canyons of the

Lehman Caves, one of the largest limestone caverns in the western United States, is now a part of Great Basin National Park. It has many decorations, including this slender column.

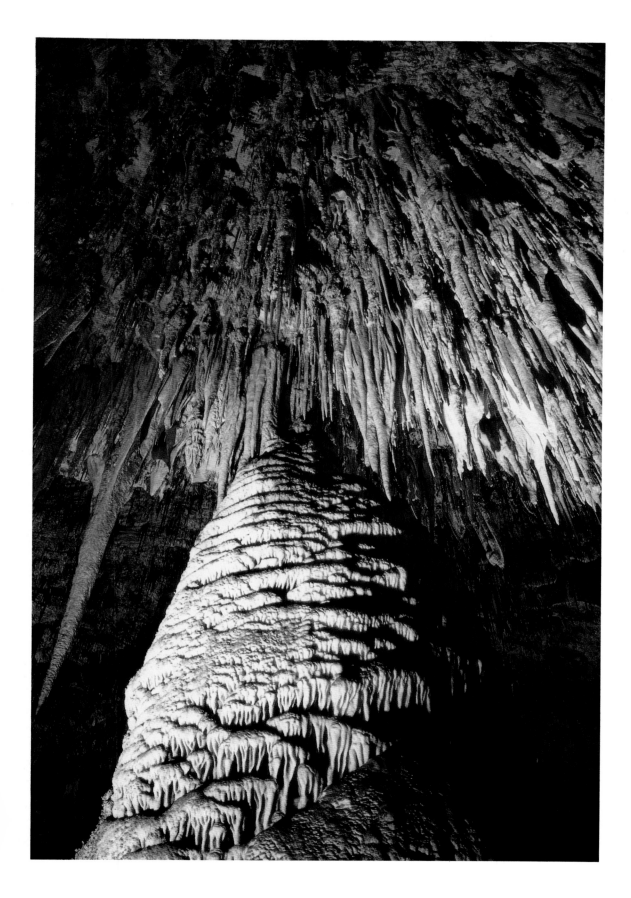

Carlsbad Caverns represents a handsome achievement in interior design, and this living room motif might be called Early Pleistocene. During the last 500,000 years mineralized water dripping into the cavern has dissolved the limestone and left hardened deposits.

A yucca grows in the dunes at White Sands National Monument in New Mexico. Plants must extend their root systems to remain atop the shifting dunes. The monument encompasses the world's largest gypsum dunefield.

The gypsum dunes at White Sands are eroded off of massive layers of gypsum rock in nearby mountains. Small animals active on the dunes have developed light coloration as a protection against predators.

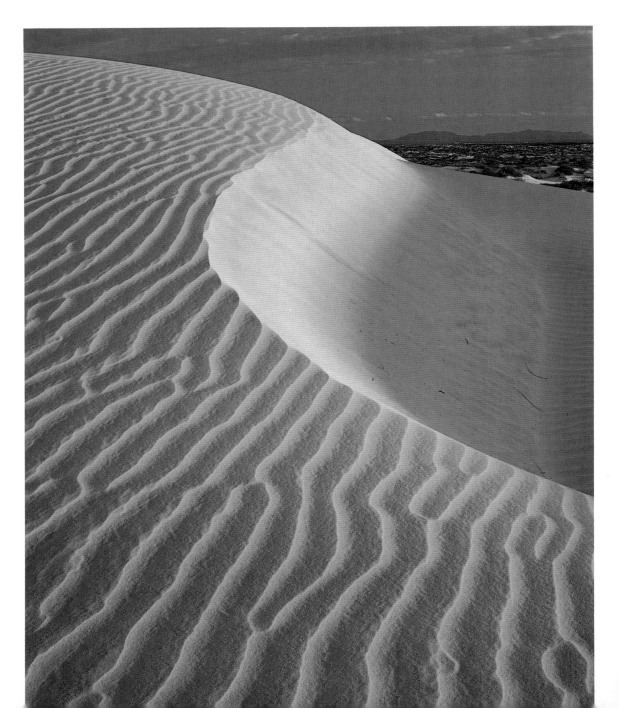

Gypsum dunes are also found in Guadalupe Mountains National Park, in western Texas.

Death Valley National Monument may be the hottest place in the United States in the summer, but snow can fall in the winter. The Panamint Range rises beyond the Racetrack on the valley floor.

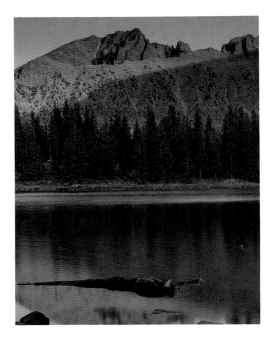

Wheeler Peak dominates the Snake Range in Great Basin National Park, the nation's 49th park, established in 1986 in eastern Nevada. The Great Basin, consisting of a sequence of thin mountain ranges and flat valleys, is one of the least visited regions of the United States.

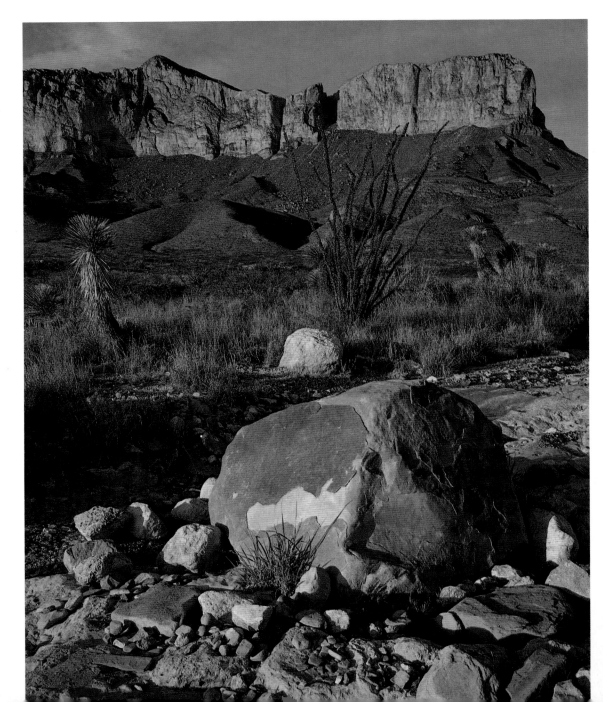

In the hard-to-believe-but-true category, the Guadalupe Mountains were originally created underwater. In the ocean, many marine organisms secreted lime that formed into limestone. The land was uplifted, the ocean disappeared, and parts of the reef are exposed to view.

Rio Grande are popular with river runners. But the park has two other "worlds," the Chihuahuan Desert and the Chisos Mountains. Taken together, the three environments provide refuge for an unusually rich flora and fauna. Nearly 400 species of birds are found here, more than in any other park. The roadrunner, preferring land to the air, hugs the ground, checking out the lizards and grasshoppers.

Spring comes early to the desert, with wildflower displays in March. The Texas bluebonnet (lupine) is prominent, and the park also contains some sixty kinds of cacti. Snakes abound, including four kinds of rattlesnakes.

Don't look for the pterosaur, however. This contemporary of the dinosaurs had a wingspread of 36 feet, and was the largest animal ever to take to the air. Alas, however, not within many millions of years.

The Great Basin is the physiographical feature occupying the state of Nevada and portions of adjacent states. Low, narrow mountain ranges rise from the otherwise flat terrain. Created when blocks of the earth's crust became faulted on both sides and were uplifted, the ranges extend from north to south and have been likened to worms crawling from Canada to Mexico. Great Basin National Park, our 49th park, was established in eastern Nevada in 1986 to preserve a portion of this environment.

It's the U-shaped loop in the Rio Grande that gives the name to Big Bend National Park in Texas. Elsewhere in the park, the river passes through deep, narrow canyons.

The moon sets at sunrise beyond Zabriskie Point in Death Valley. The valley was named by early travelers who passed through it, eager to move on.

Sand dunes add to the feeling of dryness in Death Valley. The mountains intercept the clouds and force them upward, where they release their moisture, leaving very little to reach the valley.

The Snake Range, topped off by Wheeler Peak at 13,063 feet, dominates the park. Lehman Caves, on the flank of Wheeler Peak, contains huge fluted columns of various colors. The trail to the summit of the peak passes several alpine lakes and leads to an ancient bristlecone pine forest. What was believed at that time to be the world's oldest living thing, a pine some 5,000 years old, was cut down in 1964 by a Forest Service employee who wanted to count its rings.

We cannot depart from the Great American Desert without mentioning Death Valley National Monument. Stretching down eastern California, the valley was formed when an immense block of rock sank, leaving steepcliffed mountains to the east and west. Melting ice from mountain glaciers created a lake in the valley, but the landscape remained arid because the mountains blocked the advance of clouds. The lake dried up, with its salt deposits concentrating on the desert floor. These include formations nicknamed the Devil's Golf Course, bizarre ridges, and pinnacles of salt up to three feet tall.

A spot near the pool called Badwater (don't drink from it!) is 282 feet below sea level, the lowest land in the Western Hemisphere. In summer, the valley is the hottest, driest place in the nation; a high of 134°F was once recorded—in the shade. But the valley is mild in winter, and prolific wildflower displays can occur.

On the dry desert floor of Death Valley, plants are widely placed as if in a formal garden, in order to conserve the small amount of available moisture.

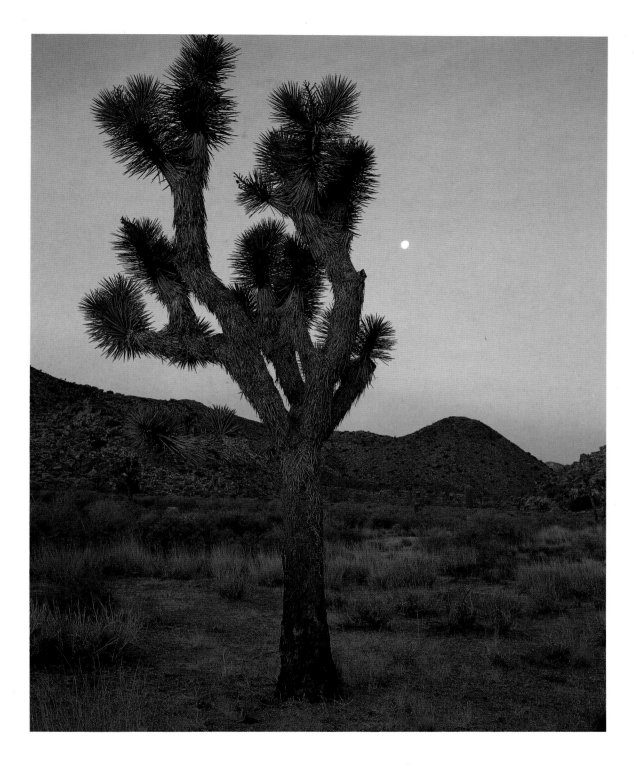

The Joshua Tree, one of nature's most whimsical concoctions, proliferates in Joshua Tree National Monument in the California desert. Mormon settlers thought the tree (actually, a yucca) resembled Joshua raising his arms to the Lord.

*e Chisos Mountains in Big Bend are a
 gh moist refuge from the low hot desert
  plants and animals. Nearly 400 species
  birds have been seen here, more than in
  y other park.*

The Golden West

Yosemite Falls, only partially visible here, is the world's second highest waterfall (2,425 feet). John Muir, first president of the Sierra Club and the leading advocate of protection for the Sierra Nevada, spoke of this park as "Holy Yosemite."

The Merced River flows through Yosemite Valley in Yosemite National Park in California. The broad, flat valley is the work of glaciers that pushed through the Sierra Nevada during the Ice Age.

The carving of glacial ice helped produce the distinctive shape of Half Dome, the tall peak in the distant right. Yosemite Valley is out of sight beyond and below the white granite surface of Yosemite's high country.

Eighty-five miles west of Badwater, Mount Whitney rises to 14,495 feet, the highest point in the United States outside Alaska. Whitney stands at the eastern boundary of Sequoia National Park, in the Sierra Nevada of California. Kings Canyon National Park adjoins Sequoia on the north. The Sierra Nevada, a shrine to John Muir and to the photographer Ansel Adams, has been called the Range of Light and the Gentle Wilderness.

Its birth was not gentle, however, occurring some 250 million years ago when the Pacific and North American plates bumped in a geological fender-bender that broke up seabed sediments and bulged them upward. The hills eroded away, but a second collision occurred 100 million years later, again even more slowly than those slow-motion crash films illustrating the efficacy of seat belts. This time the heavier Pacific plate slid under the lighter North American plate. The collision generated heat and released magma that flooded over the rocks and then cooled into granite. Further uplifting produced the near-vertical escarpment to the east, and subsequent glaciation sculptured the deep U-shaped valleys on the western slope for which the Sierra Nevada is renowned.

Clouds form above the western slope, rise, and release considerable precipitation up to about 9,000 feet. Above that the Sierra Nevada is nearly a desert. In winter snow builds up to as much as 20 feet, and the moisture released in the subsequent meltdown provides excellent conditions for the growth of giant trees. The impervious granite rock below the soil does its part, keeping the moisture accessible to even the shallow roots of the sequoias. Aside from the sequoias, other species of trees grow here to record size.

Wandering among the trees of the Giant Forest in Sequoia National Park and through sunlit meadows bordering the groves, one is humbled by the capacity of nature to create life. A tree 250 feet tall has grown from a seed so small that 90,000 of them would weigh only one pound.

No roads traverse the high country of these two parks, and this kingdom is reserved for the strong-legged children of John Muir, the inheritors of its chill beauty, of its pale granite domes and turquoise lakes and runty flowers.

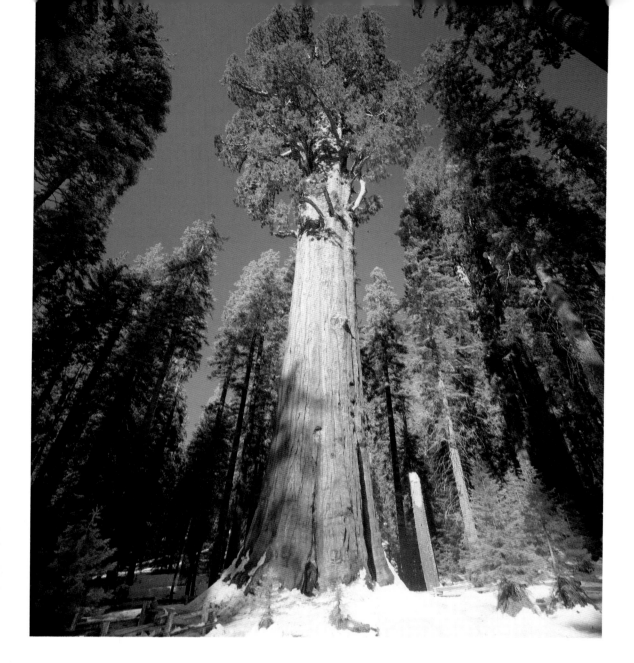

The General Sherman Tree in Sequoia National Park in the Sierra Nevada of California is the world's largest (though not tallest) living thing. This sequoia is about 2,500 years old.

Yosemite is forty miles north of Kings Canyon. The appeal of its "incomparable valley" has been duly noted. Yosemite, too, has groves of sequoias up to 2,700 years old, and its high country has earned acclaim barely secondary to the valley. Glacier Point, a lookout accessible by automobile, provides the ultimate high country "high." At your feet, a sheer cliff drops 3,200 feet to the valley. Across the valley, Yosemite Falls, the world's second highest waterfall, plunges 2,425 feet in two straight drops broken by a series of cascades. To the right, Vernal and Nevada Falls transport the waters of the Merced River down stair steps to the valley. Beyond the valley the polished peaks of the High Sierra roll on as if waves of the sea.

The Tioga Pass Road leads across the top of Yosemite, past lakes, streams, and the ubiquitous granite. Tuolumne Meadows, the Sierra's largest high-mountain meadows, is a wildflowered spread of natural beauty and a base for wilderness exploration for hikers, backpackers, and crosscountry skiers.

The coast redwoods, once widely distributed in the northern latitudes, have been in retreat for some time. The glaciers overran much of their territory, leaving a relative remnant along 450 miles of the northern California coast. Loggers, as noted, further reduced their numbers, and the surviving redwoods today are found in a checkerboard of Federal parklands and three state parks just below the Oregon border.

Fog, cool summers, and mild winters provide the climate necessary to the growth of the coast redwoods that flourish in Redwood National Park and in several California state parks. The redwoods, the world's tallest living things, grow in cathedral-like groves that leave hikers pleasantly cut off from the outside world.

As the level of Mono Lake has dropped, spires of tufa, or calcium carbonate, have appeared above the surface. The lake is east of Yosemite National Park.

At Devils Postpile National Monument, in the Sierra Nevada, basaltic lava from an eruption spread to a depth of 400 feet sometime within the last 100,000 years. Cracks occurred within the mass as it cooled and shrank. Hexagonal columns formed, and they continue to topple over.

Cool summers, abetted by fog rolling off the sea, and mild wet winters combine to provide the great amount of moisture that the trees require. Other tall trees, including hemlock, fir, and spruce, also flourish within the parks. Altogether, more than 1,000 kinds of plants and animals, including 350 birds, are found in Redwood National Park and the state parks. In a Brobdingnagian environment, even rhododendrons grow to 30 feet. The typical mature redwood may attain 200 to 250 feet in height over a lifetime of 400 to 800 years, but some individual trees live for 2,000 years, and the tallest tree has been measured at 367.8 feet. Most trails in the parks are short, but they provide a quick payoff, leading immediately into the damp, dark forest.

Sandy beaches with surf punctuated by sea stacks highlight 35 miles of coast. Majestic Roosevelt elk roam the shore and gray whales, porpoises, and seals can be sighted in the ocean.

The sheer face of El Capitan, in Yosemite Valley, has proved to be an irresistible challenge for mountain climbers.

Just 30 miles west of the teeming (with humanity) mainland of southern California, great colonies of sea mammals and sea birds flourish on Channel Islands National Park. The park is surrounded by the waters of the Channel Islands National Marine Sanctuary. The islands are an archaeological treasure, too, having been occupied by the Chumash Indians for thousands of years. Five of the eight islands are included in the park. They are accessible only by boat, and amenities are few.

Broad grasslands, high mountains with deeply cut canyons, and rolling hills are found on one or more of the islands. Steep cliffs rise from the sea. Beaches and other available nooks and crannies are occupied by wildlife. Fur-bearing mammals—otters, seals, and sea lions—have recovered from the days when they were hunted virtually to extinction. The 6,000-pound northern elephant seals form breeding colonies. Steller sea lions, California sea lions, and northern fur seals are among other animals that gather together, barking, staking out territory, and all in all creating a general uproar.

The ocean is filled with creatures ranging from the blue whale, the world's largest animal, to microscopic plankton, the bottom link of the sea world's food chain. Sea birds, including gulls, cormorants, oystercatchers, and the endangered brown pelican, also nest here. Owls, kestrels, and larks fly over from the mainland. The island fox, no bigger than a cat, roams the uplands. Stands of giant coreopsis, or "tree sunflower," up to 10 feet tall, thrive in summer.

The Channel Islands, just off the southern California coast, are dramatic landmarks and also a refuge for a great variety of bird and marine life.

Blunt headlands jut into the sea and the surf pounds against the mainland, and that's only part of the drama at Point Reyes National Seashore north of San Francisco. The San Andreas Fault, a source of devastating earthquakes, enters the ocean here as well.

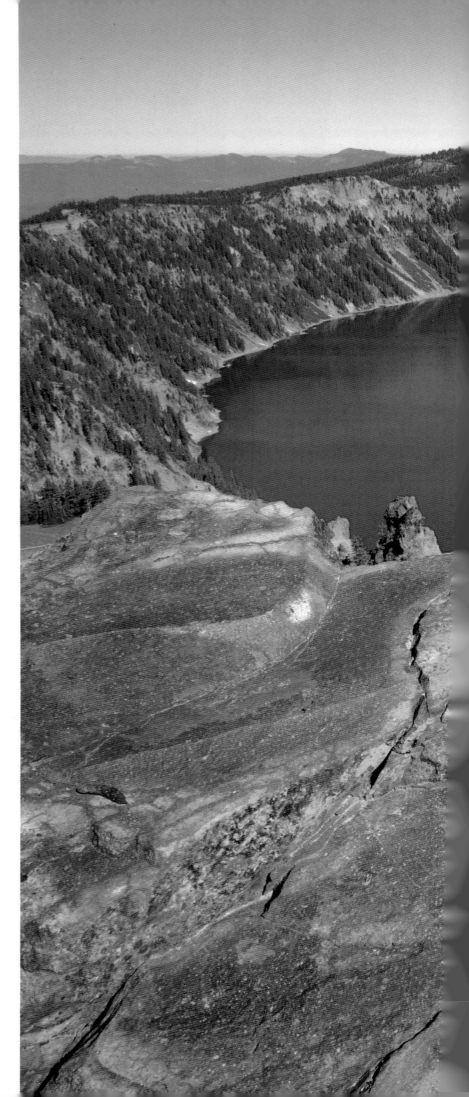

The Ring of Fire

Crater Lake, having a maximum depth of 1,932 feet, is the deepest lake in the United States. Wizard Island, rising within the lake, is itself a volcanic cone that formed after the caldera collapsed.

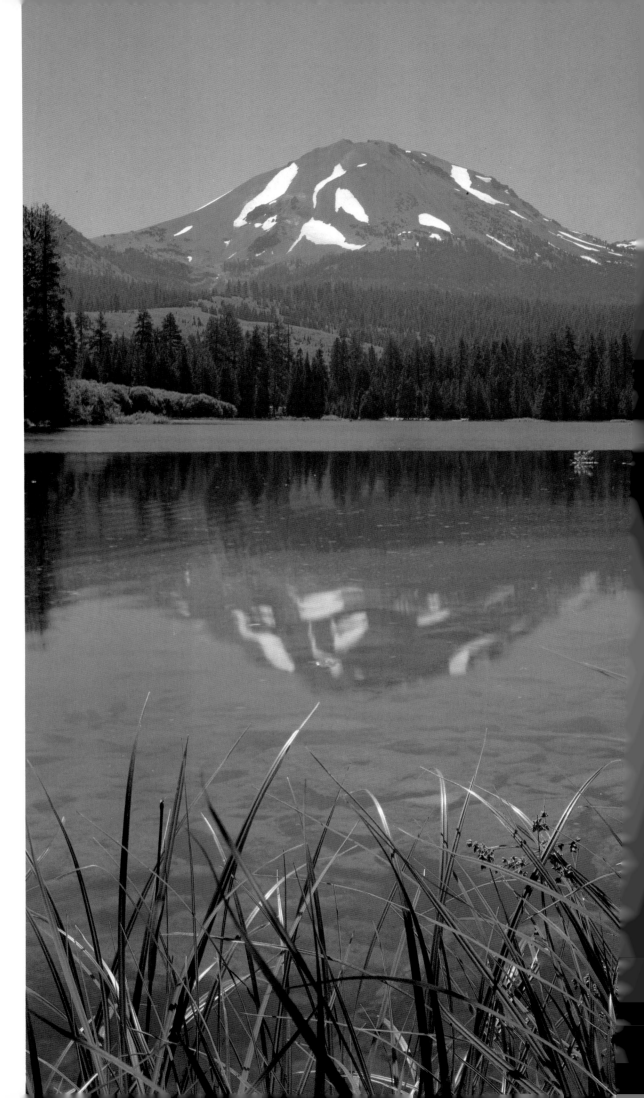

Mount Lassen in Lassen Volcanic National Park in California. Lassen was made a park after it began erupting in 1914. Like most of the volcanic areas illustrated in this section, Lassen lies on the "Ring of Fire" in the Pacific Ocean and along its rims, where plates floating on the earth's crust scrape against each other and trigger eruptions.

Haleakala National Park on the island of Maui includes this immense crater, 7.5 miles long, 2.5 miles wide, and one-half mile deep. Haleakala Crater has been dormant since about 1790, but movements of the earth underneath the ocean could produce another eruption here.

Lava pours frequently from this vent on Kilauea, one of the world's most active volcanoes. The entire chain of the Hawaii Islands is volcanic in origin. Kilauea is in fact an immense mountain that rises from the ocean floor, with 18,000 feet of it lying below the surface of the sea.

Volcanic activity can be destructive of natural environments, and also of human life and property. But the upwelling of molten rock (magma) can also be a creative force, designing mountains that resemble pyramids and distributing ash and lava that are fascinating in their own right. The world's principal volcanic zone is found along and near the rims of the Pacific ocean, at the edges of plates that compose the earth's crust. Volcanism is triggered as these great slabs override or grind past each other. As the expanding ocean crust pushes under the continental plates, it penetrates deeply enough into the earth to be partly remelted. Magma then erupts and creates volcanic mountains.

That, briefly, is the theory of plate tectonics. The reality is spectacular, all along the so-called Ring of Fire, which follows the rims of the ocean where the plates meet. Many of America's greatest natural monuments are volcanic mountains, and three volcanic national parks are found within the Pacific Ocean itself.

An aerial view of Mauna Ulu caldera, which is also visible from the Chain of Craters Road in Hawaii Volcanoes National Park. Enough lava poured from this caldera between 1969 and 1974 to add 200 acres to the island.

The National Park of American Samoa became the 50th park in 1988. The U.S. Trust Territory of American Samoa is 2,500 miles east of Australia in the South Pacific. American Samoa consists of five volcanic islands and two coral atolls, the only American soil south of the equator. The harbor and chief population center is at Pago Pago.

Volcanic activity under the ocean built up submarine mountains that eventually broke out above sea level. The largest island, Tutuila, consists of the eroded remnants of four volcanoes. Closely spaced streams have deeply eroded the mountains and left a mere skeletal backbone of mountain peaks and ridges running the length of the island. Other islands are the remnants of single volcanoes.

Days are warm and nights are balmy. Frequent rains have produced a tropical rainforest rich in flora and fauna. Two species of flying foxes, or fruit bats, may be seen by day, searching for fruit and flowers. Many birds nest along shores lined with steep cliffs inaccessible to humans. Marine life includes hawksbill turtles, who nest on the islands, and humpback whales. Snorkelers and scuba divers can explore extensive coral reefs.

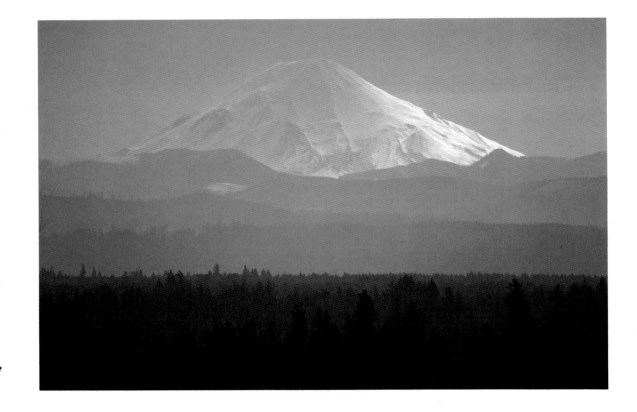

Mount St. Helens, a volcano in the Cascade Range in southern Washington state, exploded in 1980. Devastation was widespread, and more than 60 people died. Naturalists soon found, however, that plants began to struggle back atop the mass of ash and other debris.

Some 2,300 miles northeast of American Samoa, the classic chain of the Hawaiian Islands rises from the sea. Hawaii's two parks are Hawaii Volcanoes National Park on the "Big Island" of Hawaii and Haleakala National Park on Maui.

Mauna Loa and Kilauea are the active volcanoes on Hawaii. Mauna Loa and a nearby volcanic peak, Mauna Kea, both rise more than 13,000 feet above sea level. *And,* to offer a somewhat inapt metaphor, that is only the tip of the iceberg! The ocean floor lies some 18,000 feet below sea level, which means that Mauna Kea and, Mauna Loa are both more than 31,000 feet in height and are in fact considered to be the greatest mountain masses on earth. (Mount Everest is 29,028 feet above sea level.) Mauna Loa started growing three million years ago, and required the first two million years just to get as high as sea level. It has erupted hundreds of thousands of times.

Kilauea is only some 4,000 feet above sea level, but it has been extremely active (especially during the 1980s) and grows fast in geological terms. Kilauea's last truly violent eruption—accompanied by salvos of rocks, clouds of poison, and showers of hot mud—occurred in 1924. Its recent displays have been generally safe to view from a respectful distance and consist of tides of fiery red lava spilling down the slopes of the volcano. Several craters have formed on the slopes of Kilauea, and incandescent material pours from their vents.

Both Kilauea and Mauna Loa have summit basins called calderas that are two to three miles across and several hundred feet deep.

A river of lava, now solidified, pours down a slope in Craters of the Moon National Monument in Idaho, one of the eeriest landscapes in the United States. The area is dotted with small cones from which basaltic lava poured thousands of years ago.

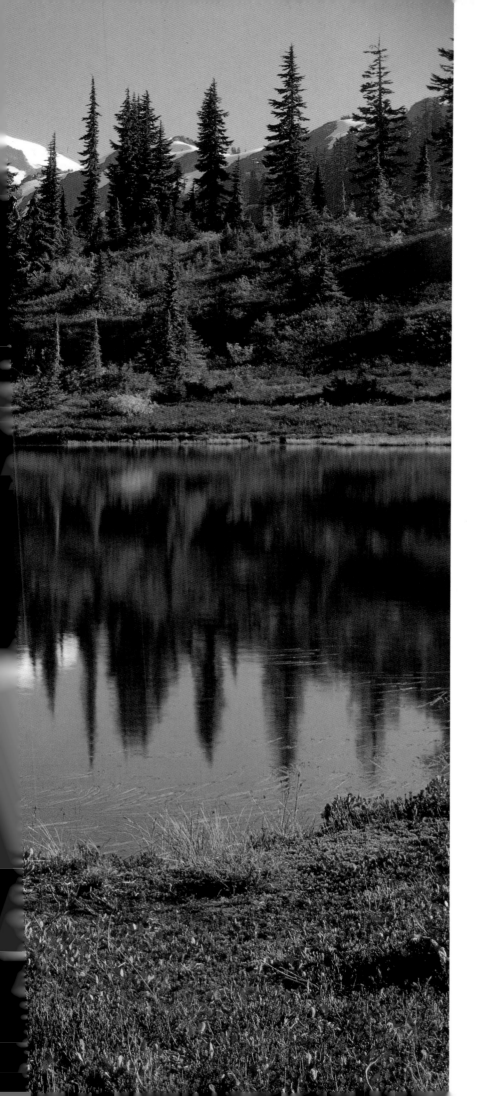

Mount Shuksan, North Cascades National Park, from Picture Lake. The park contains 318 glaciers, more than half of all found in the "Lower 48."

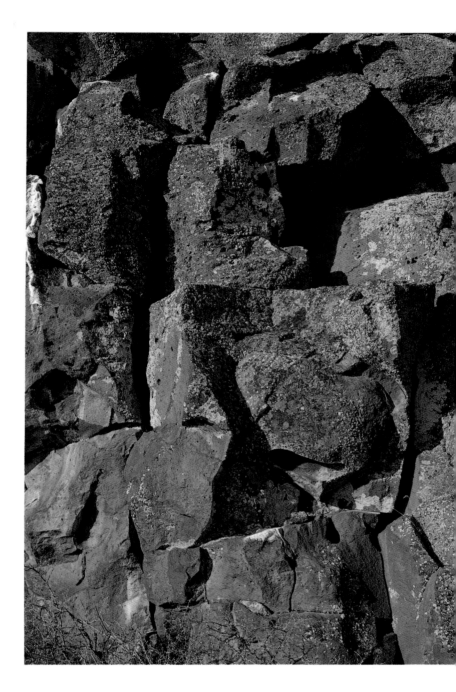

"Nature abhors a vacuum," according to the Dutch philosopher Spinoza. On the barren lava landscape of Lava Beds National Monument, in northern California, lichens represent the advance wave of the revegetation process. The lava beds spread for miles from eruptions that occurred here thousands of years ago.

This form of lava, which has cooled and solidified, is called pahoehoe. Because volcanoes in Hawaii have erupted so often, much of the land is covered by massive lava flows.

The snow-capped volcanic peak of Mount Rainier shows no symmetry after many explosions and eruptions. About 50 climbers have died trying to reach its frozen summit. The mountain's 27 glaciers constitute the largest mass of year-round ice in the United States south of Alaska. The plant in the foreground is bear grass.

Meanwhile, if you can wait, nature is building more seamounts on the ocean floor southeast of Hawaii. One is 15,000 feet high, or just 3,000 feet below sea level. Humanoids of the distant future will attend Rotary conventions there and loll on its sandy beaches.

The winds and the digestive tracts of birds transported spores and seeds of plants to the islands, and the Hawaiian Islands, because of their isolation, developed a unique flora and fauna. Some seventy species of native birds evolved from about fifteen species that made it to the island from elsewhere. The Hawaiian goose, or nene, a ground-nesting bird that prefers to live on lightly vegetated lava flows, was brought to the point of extinction by rats and mongooses taken to the islands by humans. But it appears to be recovering.

The centerpiece of Haleakala National Park is Haleakala Crater, 7.5 miles long, 2.5 miles wide, and one-half mile deep. Haleakala last erupted about 1790, not too long ago in volcanic terms, and it is probably not extinct, just dormant.

The most famous plant of the crater is the silversword, a two-foot-wide rosette with many dagger-like silvery leaves. Too attractive for its own good—humans pulled them up and goats ate them—the silverswords were near extinction at one time but they are now recovering under protection of the park. Once in its lifetime the silversword sends up a cluster of 100 to 500 yellow and purplish flowers on a stalk up to eight feet tall—and then the plant dies.

In contrast to the ash and lava-covered surface of the crater, the Kipahulu section of the park offers rolling grasslands and forested valleys that drop sharply to the sea. The upper rain forest receives as much as 250 inches of rain a year. A chain of pools connected with waterfalls and cascades lead from the forest to the ocean.

On the U.S. mainland, the Cascade Mountains trace the path of the Ring of Fire through the Pacific Northwest. The southernmost volcano in the Cascades is Lassen Peak in northern California. Lassen Volcanic National Park was established in 1916 even as eruptions were continuing. The biggest explosion in a four-year sequence (1914-1917) occurred on May 22, 1915, when a release of lava and gas sent a mushroom cloud seven miles into the stratosphere.

Lassen, which had erupted many times, began as a vent on the flank of Mount Tehama, an immense volcano whose peak collapsed a long time ago into its own caldera. Though Lassen has remained quiet since a few final puffs in 1921, it is certainly not extinct. Meanwhile, scientists study the recovery of plant species in this outdoor laboratory. The young forest has proved in places to be even more diverse than the adult forest wiped out by the eruptions.

Tracing the Cascades to the north, the next park is in Oregon—Crater Lake, atop Mount Mazama, which William Steel had successfully promoted as a park.

In southern Washington state, Mount St. Helens was just one of many lovely snow-capped Cascade peaks until May 18, 1980, when a volcanic explosion of unimaginable force blew off the top 1,300 feet of the mountain and lofted a plume of smoke and ash fifteen miles into the sky. A tide of glowing gas and rock and thick mud swept down the slopes, obliterating 200 square miles of timber, lakes, and valley. Spirit Lake, a popular recreation area, became a desert. More than 60 persons died. Mount St. Helens National Volcanic Monument was established under the administration of the U.S. Forest Service.

The crowning glory of the Cascade Range is Mount Rainier, the beloved symbol of Washington state, rising 14,410 feet in isolated splendor, its snowfields visible from all directions for one hundred miles. Residents of Seattle and Tacoma may be forgiven for casting nervous glances at the volcano articulating their skyline. Rainier erupted in the 1800s and many times before that. Once, geologists believe, its peak was a perfect Mt. Fuji-style cone reaching to 16,000 feet in elevation, but ice sheets and an eruption some 5,800 years ago knocked off some of the summit and marred the symmetry. Twenty-seven glaciers have cut deeply into the slopes of Rainier, and they are separated by rock walls called cleavers.

Moist air flowing off the Pacific encounters nothing like this mountain. Clouds form and surrender about 100 inches of precipitation a year, mostly in the form of snow. The three-story Paradise Inn, a popular spot for visitors in summer, may be buried up to its roof. In the spring, meltwater

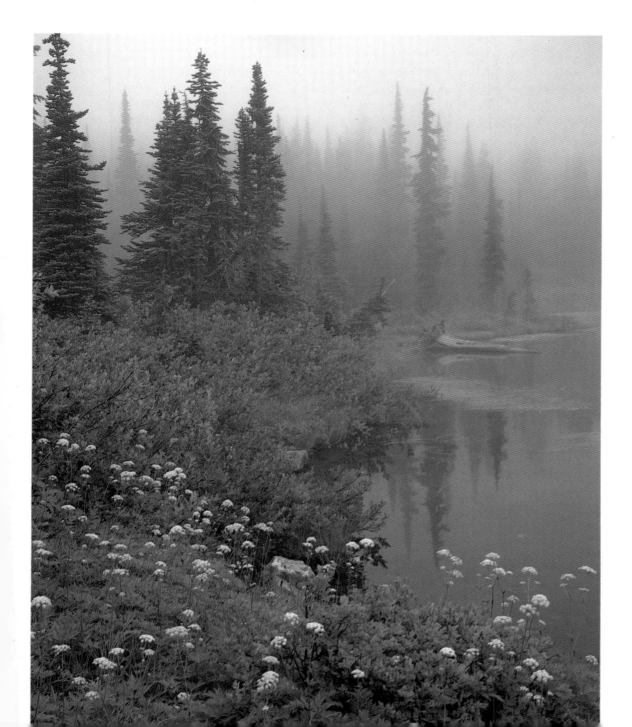

The deep, lush virgin forest on the slopes of Mount Rainier in Washington becomes a fantasyland when shrouded in fog that closes off the outside world. This is Reflection Lake.

Soleduck Falls is in the heart of the Olympic National Park rain forest. Thirteen rivers flow from the mountains to the sea. The forest is the best surviving remnant of the primeval rain forests of the Northwest that have now been so extensively logged.

pours off the mountain, in places carving otherworldly ice caves, enchanting in their light and pale blue color.

At lower elevations, Douglas fir, red cedars, and western hemlock rise 200 feet in a massive forest. Above the trees, the subalpine landscape offers colorful displays of raw beauty and open views of wildlife, including the delightful marmots, furry rodents who romp about, watch, whistle, and look over their two-footed visitors.

Volcanism played a role in the creation of the Olympic Range, now partly within Olympic National Park west of Seattle. The future home of the gods, Mount Olympus and its neighbors got their start 55 million years ago on the floor of the Pacific Ocean. Massive amounts of sediments were washed into the sea and compressed into shale and sandstone. Lava joined this mix, pouring forth from fissures in the earth's crust, and hardening into basalt. Underwater mountains—seamounts—formed. Later, the Pacific plate bearing these submerged mountains collided with the continental plate, another exciting physiographic event we missed by a mere 30 million years. A portion of the seamounts slid under the continental plate, but their tops piled up to become today's Olympic Range. Glaciers, the last of which retreated 12,000 years ago, designed the present pattern of peaks and valleys. The glaciers carved Juan de Fuca Strait and Puget Sound, nearly isolating the Olympics from the mainland.

The Olympics form a tight cluster, from which thirteen rivers tumble to the sea like spokes of a wheel. They are supplied by up to 200 inches of annual precipitation. That's on the western side. The eastern side is nearly a desert.

A temperate rain forest, the nation's finest example, spreads westward at low elevations from the mountains to the Pacific Ocean. Sitka spruce is the principal tree of the forest. The dense canopy of trees catches snow that never reaches the ground. A carpet of moss absorbs sound, and the ambience in the subdued light is that of a cathedral. The composition of the forest changes with increases in elevation, and above the tree line the subalpine zone features flower-floored meadows.

Wildlife includes the shy Roosevelt elk, travelling in elusive herds, and mountain goats, an introduced species that seems to eat everything in sight. The Park Service is trying to figure out how to get rid of them.

The park encompasses 57 miles of Pacific coastline. Sea stacks rise from the ocean, and the forest nearly meets the sea, enhancing the drama of this wild, isolated world of contact and conflict. Bears cruise the beach in search of food. Raccoons feed on shellfish at low tide. Birds are everywhere, inspecting what the sea has thrown them. Eagles circle overhead, oystercatchers pry open mussels with their long bills, and turnstones turn stones in search of goodies underneath. Gulls drop clamshells from a height of 50 feet to crack them open on rocks.

Seattle invariably ranks near the top of lists naming the "best" places to live in the United States. Parklands nearly surround the city. The most rugged wilderness is found in the North Cascades National Park Service Complex northeast of Seattle. The complex includes the park as well as Ross Lake and Lake Chelan national recreation areas.

Complex is also a good word for the jumbled landforms of the North Cascades. A sort of geological tossed salad, the mountains offer up scenery for which no other experience has prepared the visitor. The writer and photographer Kim Heacox has observed, "Adjectives that worked elsewhere failed here, as if our language had evolved in a world without comparable scenery." Others have called the North Cascades the American Alps.

North Cascades National Park in Washington is a mecca for serious mountain climbers. The region, which has a geologically complex history, has been called the American Alps.

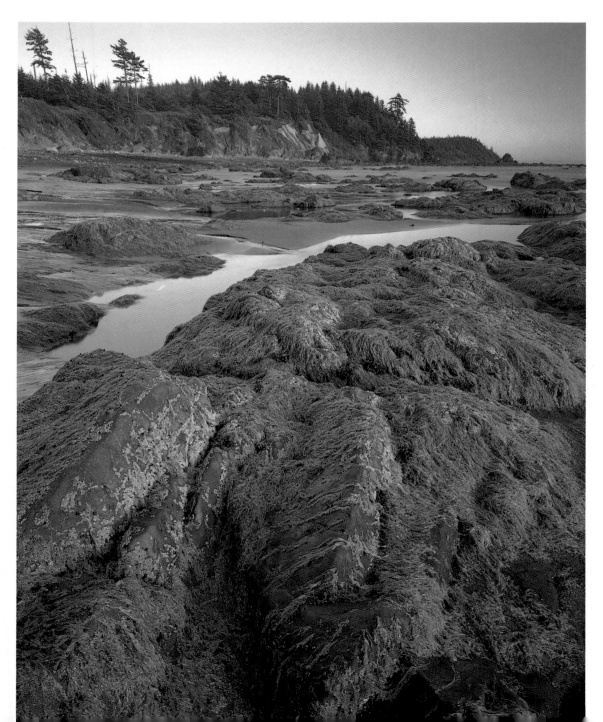

A winter storm flogs the beach in Olympic National Park. Incoming tides have trapped visitors hiking around headlands along the shore.

The Olympic Shore in Washington State is wild, rugged, and isolated, and 57 miles of it are included in Olympic National Park. Marine organisms occupy its pools at low tide, and birds and beasts of the nearby forests come to the coast in search of food. This is near Cape Alava.

131

To make a very long story short, sediments laid down half a billion years ago were rearranged by volcanism, erosion, and the movement of the earth's plates. Shallow seas depositing sediments covered what was left. The cycle of mountain building and erosion repeated itself several times. Magma burst out of the earth and spilled over the terrain, and two volcanic lava mountains, Baker and Glacier Peak (both outside the park) rose above the Cascade summits. The icefields moved in and out, leaving 318 glaciers in the park. The mountains are nearly impenetrable, and few people knew much about them before the park was established in 1968. The hardy few included members of mountain-climbing clubs.

The densely conifered western slope gets 110 inches of precipitation a year, yet a valley just to the east of the park gets only twelve inches. Major mammals, including mountain lions, bobcats, black bears, and mule deer, are well represented.

State Route 20 cuts through the complex to the reservoirs in the recreation areas and provides access to many trails leading into the wilderness. The glacier-carved and pencil-shaped Lake Chelan, 55 miles long and 1,500 feet deep, points into the wilderness. The trip up the lake and into the beyond is an exceptional experience.

The National Park of American Samoa became America's 50th park in 1988. In Samoan legend, these two islets off the island of Tutuila represent two lovers.

Crater Lake, in the collapsed caldera of Mount Mazama, formed after a volcanic eruption 7,000 years ago. Ash spread across eight states and three Canadian provinces.

133

Alaska

Unlike humans, brown (grizzly) bears need no fishing license at the Brooks River in Katmai National Park. The annual summer salmon run brings out the bears in force, providing one of the best opportunities anywhere to observe North America's largest land predator in action.

A caribou roams the high country in Denali National Park and Preserve. This Park has large populations of caribou, moose, grizzly bear, and Dall sheep, many of which can be observed easily from the park road.

White icebergs, a blue glacier, and dark mountains combine in an exceptional scene further punctuated with the bright red of beach peas. This is Kenai Fjords National Park, another frozen fastness that tantalizes the adventurous.

Early people called it Alyeshka—"The Great Land." Our northern subcontinent wins the gold in almost every competition in America's Landscape Olympics. Alaska has the biggest moose and bears, the tallest spruce, the tallest mountains, the largest glaciers, and simply more of almost every landform.

The land's youthful energy can be felt and measured, in mountains still pushing upward, in undammed rivers running free to the ocean, in the unrestrained movement of animal life—streambeds turn red with salmon, caribou flow across the tundra, mobs of mosquitoes persecute the caribou.

Glacier Bay National Park, in the panhandle of southeast Alaska, may be changing more rapidly than any of America's other crown jewels. Reminiscent of the dog that didn't bark, this is a story of the glacier that's not there.

The story begins with the start of the Little Ice Age about 4,000 years ago. Glaciers formed as snowfall in the mountains exceeded snowmelt. Snowflakes changed to round ice grains and then, under mounting weight, to solid ice. Gravity moved the mass downslope, perhaps a few feet per day. Glaciers advanced in this area until about 1750, and then a meltdown began. The snout (front) of the bay's glacier began to retreat up the bay. When observed in 1794, Glacier Bay's snout still reached nearly to its mouth. No small affair, this glacier was 4,000 feet thick and up to 20 miles wide, and it extended upbay more than 100 miles to the mountains.

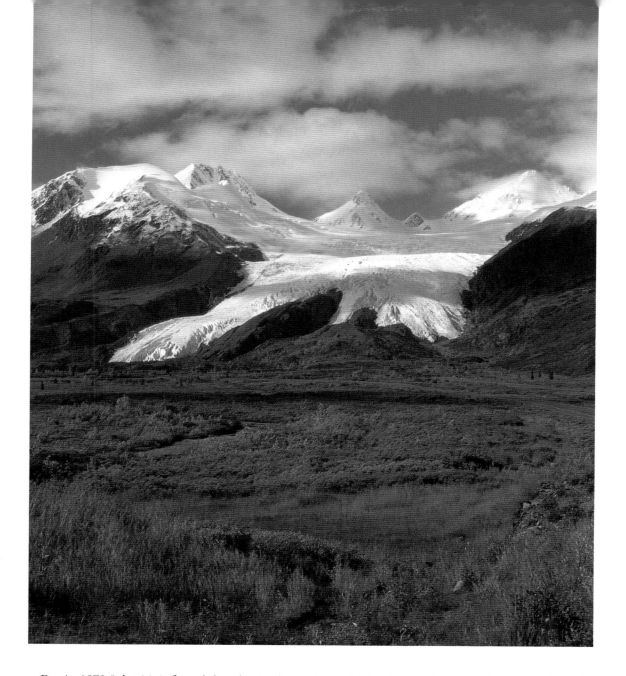

Wrangell-St. Elias, the nation's largest national park, contains massive ice fields and glaciers that are nearly inaccessible but a wonder to behold. The world's tallest coastal mountains and miles-wide braided rivers are among the features of this outsized landscape.

But in 1879 John Muir found that the ice had retreated 48 miles up the bay. Glacier Bay branches like a tree into a number of inlets, and most of their respective glaciers continue to fall back. No other glacier has been known to retreat so fast, and scientists are studying how this process may be related to subtle changes in climate.

The calving of glaciers is one of nature's showiest performances. Slabs of ice up to 200 feet high break loose and crash into the water. An underwater slab may pop off, rush to the surface, and capsize unwary boaters.

From mountain tundra to the hemlock and spruce forest, the park provides sanctuary for a broad range of plants and animals. For most visitors, the biggest thrill is seeing a humpback whale, up to 50 feet long, surface briefly in the bay, then dive, its tail flukes standing tall for an instant before it disappears. Whales sing to each other, and maybe someday we will be able to decode their messages.

Northwest of Glacier Bay, where Alaska's panhandle joins the pan, Wrangell-St. Elias National Park and Preserve soars out of the Gulf of Alaska. Six times the size of Yellowstone, Wrangell-St. Elias is by far the nation's largest park. Its other superlatives include the Bagley Ice Field, 80 miles long, and the nation's two biggest glaciers—one of them the size of Rhode Island—which it feeds. The St. Elias Mountains, with Mount Logan over the border in Canada reaching to 19,850 feet, are the world's tallest coastal mountains. Canyons rival Yosemite and Zion in size. The mineral wealth was bountiful. Silver was extensively mined in the future park, and the famed Kennecott mine, until it closed in 1938, yielded one billion pounds of copper.

The mighty Copper River forms the western boundary of Wrangell-St. Elias, and a major tributary, the glacier-fed Chitina River, is a superlative example of its own kind. The Chitina flows from east to west, and its valley provides access by gravel road to the center of the park. Within its broad valley bottom, the Chitina spreads several miles wide, following a complex vine of channels and creating a classic Alaskan braided river.

Compact bands of the majestic all-white Dall sheep roam the high meadows and inhospitable ridgetops. As in other parks bearing the designation, the "preserve" sections are open to sport hunting of the sheep and other wildlife.

Rafting, hiking, cross-country skiing, and fishing opportunities are available, but much of this park is an unapproachable (for most of us) and icebound wilderness, and you might prefer just to stay home and watch the video.

Kenai Fjords National Park, on the Gulf of Alaska's west coast, is, in one way, a junior version of Wrangell. Its dominant feature is the Harding Ice Field, 300 square miles spread across the Kenai Mountains. The mountains are nearly buried, their summits barely above the white sheets. The icefield is sustained by up to 600 inches of annual snowfall.

Anyone planning a trek across the icefield should prepare for sudden storms, high winds, extreme temperature changes, and blinding sunlight bouncing off the snow. That's in the summer, when the going is easiest. In other seasons you might encounter real problems. And watch out for those nasty crevasses.

Tectonic plates collide along the coast, and, as one slides under the other, Kenai's coast is being dragged underwater, and the mountains now tilt into the sea. As alpine valleys fill with seawater, they become fjords, and these fingers of the gulf reach far inland. In a violent land, change can come quickly. In 1964 an earthquake twice as powerful as the 1906 San Francisco shocker devastated the nearby town of Seward and dropped the Kenai shoreline six feet in one day!

Bears prowl the narrow inhabitable strip of coast, and sea life in quantity occupies the shore and the nearby islands. Sea otters, once hunted nearly to extinction, cavort in protected safety. About 175,000 seabirds have staked out their turf and cling to their few rocky inches of the American

Mount McKinley rises more than three miles above its base, a distance unequaled by any mountain anywhere, and this contributes to its tremendous visual power. Unfortunately, in summer, McKinley is lost in the clouds more than half the time.

The East Fork of the Tolkat River spreads across its valley in Denali. Its waters choose first one channel, then another, and in spring perhaps all of them. These braided rivers, unable to cut deep channels because of the underlying permafrost, are a special feature of Alaskan landscapes.

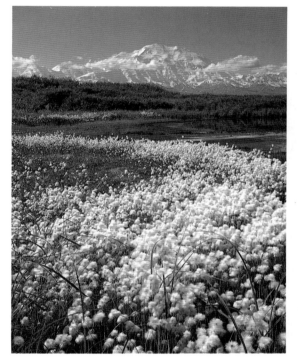

Taiga is a Russian word meaning "land of little sticks." The taiga is a familiar feature in Denali and elsewhere in Alaska. The "sticks" are short trees, such as these conifers, that would grow much taller in soils having more nutrients.

During the long dark winter, the tundra beneath Mount McKinley seems nearly lifeless, but warm weather brings out masses of blossoms. This is cotton grass.

Dream. Gulls, puffins, and kittiwakes put on quite a show, and bald eagles nest in the tops of spruce and hemlock trees.

Prince William Sound lies to the northeast, and the calamitous oil spill there in 1989 spread south toward the Kenai coast, with devastating consequences for its wildlife.

The peaks of the Aleutian Range are anchored to the mainland to the east, and to the west they dip into the sea as the Aleutian Islands. These are restless, living mountains, very much a part of the Ring of Fire. Near the head of the Aleutian Peninsula, a week of earthquakes in early June 1912 had signaled disquiet down below, and the few people living in the immediate area cleared out.

But the sunny morning of June 6 gave no promise that darkness would fall at the noon hour, that the most violent day on earth in the last 3,500 years of recorded history was at hand. At 1 p.m., with a thunderclap of sound heard 700 miles away, a small vent at the foot of Mount Katmai began to eject seven cubic miles of volcanic vomit, a flood of incandescent sand and gas that inundated, to a depth of 700 feet, a valley fifteen miles long and three to six miles wide.

A black tide of airborne ash rolled southeast. At a fishing camp 30 miles distant, a man wrote his wife, "We are awaiting death at any minute…Here are darkness and hell, thunder and noise. I do not know whether it is day or night." In Kodiak, 100 miles from Mount Katmai, a lantern held at arm's length could not be seen for two days. The eruption, ten times more powerful than the one at Mount St. Helens, hazed most of the Northern Hemisphere, and the reduced sunshine cooled the summer.

Members of a National Geographic Society expedition found a crater lake on Mount Katmai and thought that the summit was the source of the eruption. Not so, however. Most of the release came from Novarupta, a mere pimple at the edge of the valley, just 200 feet high. Magma ejected from Novarupta was drained from under Mount Katmai, whose summit then subsided, leaving the caldera in which the lake formed.

The volcanic ash and sand that spread across the valley interacted with buried rivers to produce one of nature's most sinister spectacles. Everywhere one looked, steam rose from vents in the ground in this (newly named) Valley of Ten Thousand Smokes. The smoke fizzled out within thirty years, and the volcanic deposits consolidated into tuff, a form of soft rock. Creeks have cut deep canyons within the tuff. But Novarupta still exhales steam from its mouth, its breathing as ominous as that of a horror film slasher.

No one died as a result of the eruption. Today this great park, accessible only by plane and boat, is an untouched wilderness, ruled by the nation's largest grizzlies (because they dine on salmon). At up to 1,500 pounds, they are the world's largest predators on land. In one of nature's most dramatic demonstrations of the power of instinct, salmon return from the sea by the millions, stop eating, turn red in color, and swim up rivers to the graveled streambeds of their birth, to spawn and die and provide food for bears and eagles.

The wildlife in the park's lakes and forests and along its many bayfronts is bountiful. Katmai has room for one to roam, to inhale the freshness of unsullied nature and to experience what the writer Susan Tollefson has called "the feeling—that indescribable feeling—one has when traveling alone and unarmed through raw, rugged, unpeopled country."

The Ring of Fire continues to the northeast of Katmai, and some of its major ramparts are included in Lake Clark National Park and Preserve. The mountains in the park are the Chigmits, products of various geological processes. Two active volcanoes, Iliamna and Redoubt, let off steam from time to time.

The park was established in part to protect the sockeye salmon, which make their annual "run" here in prodigious numbers, some 35 million in 1981, for example. Showing an unhuman ability to meet deadlines—and this is their ultimate deadline—the sockeye assemble off the coast in early summer, having swum from thousands of miles away. They proceed to Iliamna Lake and then to the particular streambed where they were spawned.

This roadless wilderness of tundra, lake, and forest actually has a short trail, which leads from Lake Clark, near the airstrip, to Tanalian Falls, four miles round-trip. Other than that, you're on your own, through fields of boulders, bogs, quicksand, and slippery slopes. This excursion is not for the inexperienced, or for anyone incapable of experiencing a transcendant moment. Three of the nation's officially designated wild rivers are within the park, and they lead floating transients past moose and beaver dams, waterfalls and waterfowl sanctuaries, and down challenging rapids.

Still farther north, the Aleutian Range terminates, jammed up against the Alaska Range, the 600-mile arc of mountains that separates south central Alaska from the interior plateau to the north. The Alaska Range formed along the path of the Denali Fault, where the earth buckled, fractured, and folded. Blocks of the crust lifted up to form mountains, and underneath a chamber of magma cooled gradually into granite. The granite, too, was pushed up, breaching the surface and forming an awesome massif that ultimately surpassed the older mountains.

The colossus that rises in lofty isolation from its neighbors, more than three miles above its base, was called Denali, "the High One," by the Athabascans. The name is perpetuated in "Denali National Park and Preserve," but the mountain itself bears the name given it in 1896 by a prospector, as a tribute to a senator who had just been nominated for president, William McKinley.

Ice, hundreds of feet thick in places, overlies the granite core of Mount McKinley. Permanent snowfields cover more than half of the mountain, and glaciers carve its flanks. A temperature of -95°F has been recorded on the mountain, and winds can gust to 150 miles an hour. More often than not in summer, the High One is concealed behind a cloud cover.

The many glaciers that flow off Mount McKinley and its neighbors feed magnificent examples of braided rivers, which spread out across valleys, unable to form deep channels because of the underlying permafrost.

In the lowlands, the principal ecological divisions are taiga and tundra. Taiga, a Russian word, means "land of little sticks." The sticks, which flourish mostly in the river valleys, are stunted versions of aspen, birch, poplar, and spruce. Above the valleys, the tundra begins at elevations of 2,000 feet. Here, dwarfed shrubs and miniaturized flowers adjust to the short growing season. Despite their small size, they are vitally important as a source of nutrients for the wildlife.

Because of the vast open terrain (in a park larger than Massachusetts), wildlife can be seen easily. Herds of caribou often approach the park road, while the solitary moose feeds on willows along streams. Wolves are about, but more wary. Dall sheep, their white coats and yellow horns

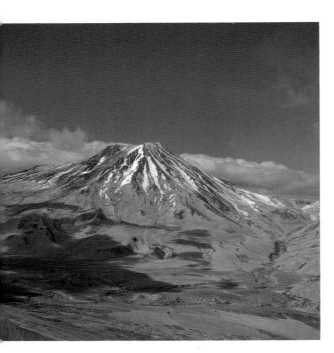

Katmai National Park was the scene, in 1912, of the most powerful volcanic eruption since 1500 B.C., but the destructive flood of ash and hot glowing pumice did not come from the summit of Mount Katmai (shown here) but from a small cone nearby called Novarupta.

A scenic climax of sorts occurs north of the Arctic Circle, in Gates of the Arctic National Park and Preserve. In a vast inland empire of mountain and valley, of river and tundra, lovers of nature who have explored all other landscapes and met all other challenges outdoors can visit this wilderness at the edge of the world and rejoice at the freedom it confers upon us.

Lake Clark National Park and Preserve is a roadless and nearly trailless region where backpackers can roam virtually at will for weeks through flowered alpine tundra and rolling hills, and past pristine lakes and smoking volcanoes.

making them one of nature's handsomest animals, negotiate the high rocky slopes. Omnivorous grizzly bears, consuming plants, berries, squirrels, moose, caribou calves and carrion with equal gusto, ramble through the park.

A few bird species, including raven, ptarmigan, magpie, and gray jay, winter here, but most birds stay only for the summer. In what has to be the world's longest commute, the Arctic tern flies in each year from Antarctica.

Four park areas lie north of the Arctic Circle. In the west, bordering Kotzebue Sound, Cape Krusenstern National Monument protects the sites of artifacts that trace the history of human hunting of marine mammals over a span of 6,000 years. Noatak National Preserve contains the nation's largest untouched river basin. Flowing from glacial melt on Mount Igikpak in the Brooks Range, the Noatak River has cut the scenic Grand Canyon of the Noatak, a migration route for animals and canoeists and kayakers who float placidly in summer and camp at "night" under the midnight sun.

Waterborne travel on the Kobuk and Salmon rivers is de rigeur in Kobuk Valley National Park, which is served by no dirt roads, much less an interstate highway. Mountains bracket the valley, but the river brings explorers close to the park's most unusual feature—the Great Kobuk Sand Dunes, 25 square miles of rounded, frosted grains of quartzite and other minerals. The dune field, the largest above the Arctic Circle, seems Arizonan in summer when temperatures can hit 100°F. Dunes rise to 100 feet.

The tide of barren-ground caribou crosses the Kobuk River twice yearly, and for an astonishing 12,500 years—according to archaeological evidence—humans have been waiting at a place called Onion Portage to kill a few of the animals for food and clothing. This use of the caribou by Natives on a subsistence basis is still allowed.

The Brooks Range, running west from Canada, is the northernmost extension of the Rocky Mountains, and a portion of the central Brooks Range lies within Gates of the Arctic National Park and Preserve. The National Park Service calls Gates of the Arctic "America's ultimate wilderness." Encompassing 8,400,000 acres, much of it in gentle valleys, Gates has more explorable land than any other park. The exploration does not come without planning, however. Aside from an absence of roads, there aren't even any trails in a park 200 miles wide, and access is by charter plane.

Such prominent spires as Mount Igikpak and the Arrigetch Peaks are formed in granite, the product of volcanic action, but many other summits are in limestone. The comings and goings of the glacial sheets have left a sculptured wonderland of U-shaped valleys, hanging valleys, tarns and cirques. Moraines have helped form mountain lakes. Runoff from rain spills swiftly over the permanently frozen ground.

Robert Marshall, a founder of the Wilderness Society who explored the Brooks Range in the 1930s and wrote lyrically in its behalf, came up with the idea for the park's name. He saw two massive peaks, Frigid Crags and Boreal Mountain, stationed on either side of the North Fork of the Koyukuk River, as the gates to the northland.

Taiga gives way on the north slope of the Brooks Range to tundra that stretches up to the Arctic Ocean, a carpet of heath, grass, sedge, moss, and lichen in never-ending patterns of growth. The flowering season is brief but intense. Although the caribou herds pass this way, too, animal life is otherwise widely distributed because of the scarcity of edible plants. But 130 kinds of birds have been seen, and trout, grayling, and pike are found in the lakes and streams.

After fingering those glossy brochures describing the delights of Acapulco, consider a park that has something for everyone: perpetual daylight, perpetual darkness, temperatures ranging from 90°F to -70°F, wolves, bears, rainbows, the aurora borealis, and an absolute freedom most people have never known. In truth the park *is* for everyone, and not just for those few who commit themselves to it physically. New Yorkers who don't even get to the Statue of Liberty want to know that it is there, and we all need to know that a place like Gates of the Arctic is there, an escape of last resort from whatever stress civilization has imposed upon us, a gift to ourselves to cherish and treasure forever.

In Glacier Bay, ice meets water and tidewater glaciers reach down to the sea. Large slabs of ice frequently calve, or break off, from the glaciers and crash into the water.

At dusk and moonrise, Mount McKinley, in Denali National Park and Preserve, dwarfs the mountains in the foreground. "The High One," as Native Americans call it, rises 20,320 feet, the tallest peak in North America.

McBride Glacier in Glacier Bay National Park, Alaska. McBride is among the glaciers that have been retreating in the park, apparently as the result of subtle changes in climate.